HowExpert G
Skiing and Snow

101 Tips to Learn How to Choose Your Equipment, Find the Best Slopes, and Ski & Snowboard for Fun, Fitness, and Fulfillment

HowExpert with Blake Randall

Copyright HowExpert™
www.HowExpert.com

For more tips related to this topic, visit HowExpert.com/skiing

Recommended Resources

- HowExpert.com – Quick 'How To' Guides on All Topics from A to Z by Everyday Experts.
- HowExpert.com/free – Free HowExpert Email Newsletter.
- HowExpert.com/books – HowExpert Books
- HowExpert.com/courses – HowExpert Courses
- HowExpert.com/clothing – HowExpert Clothing
- HowExpert.com/membership – HowExpert Membership Site
- HowExpert.com/affiliates – HowExpert Affiliate Program
- HowExpert.com/jobs – HowExpert Jobs
- HowExpert.com/writers – Write About Your #1 Passion/Knowledge/Expertise & Become a HowExpert Author.
- HowExpert.com/resources – Additional HowExpert Recommended Resources
- YouTube.com/HowExpert – Subscribe to HowExpert YouTube.
- Instagram.com/HowExpert – Follow HowExpert on Instagram.
- Facebook.com/HowExpert – Follow HowExpert on Facebook.
- TikTok.com/@HowExpert – Follow HowExpert on TikTok.

Publisher's Foreword

Dear HowExpert Reader,

HowExpert publishes quick 'how to' guides on all topics from A to Z by everyday experts.

At HowExpert, our mission is to discover, empower, and maximize everyday people's talents to ultimately make a positive impact in the world for all topics from A to Z...one everyday expert at a time!

All of our HowExpert guides are written by everyday people just like you and me, who have a passion, knowledge, and expertise for a specific topic.

We take great pride in selecting everyday experts who have a passion, real-life experience in a topic, and excellent writing skills to teach you about the topic you are also passionate about and eager to learn.

We hope you get a lot of value from our HowExpert guides, and it can make a positive impact on your life in some way. All of our readers, including you, help us continue living our mission of positively impacting the world for all spheres of influences from A to Z.

If you enjoyed one of our HowExpert guides, then please take a moment to send us your feedback from wherever you got this book.

Thank you, and we wish you all the best in all aspects of life.

Sincerely,

BJ Min
Founder & Publisher of HowExpert
HowExpert.com

PS...If you are also interested in becoming a HowExpert author, then please visit our website at HowExpert.com/writers. Thank you & again, all the best!

Table of Contents

Recommended Resources..................................... 2

Publisher's Foreword 3

Chapter 1: Hey Kid, Wanna Hit the Slopes? 7

Gear Up!...7

   Tailor Your Experience Like a Fine Suit.....................7

   Lay of the Land.. 11

   Reasons Behind the Recs....................................18

   Brand Recommendations................................... 26

   One Last Story 34

The Foundation on Top of the Foundation 38

   If the Boot Fits, It Also Binds 38

Style Isn't Everything, Warmth Is 45

   Dress for Success 45

Chapter Review: 51

Chapter 2: Easier to Learn, but Harder to Master

.... 52

Earn Your Turns 52

   If You Pizza, When You Need to French Fry, You're
Gonna Have a Bad Time...52

Chapter Review: 69

Chapter 3: Harder to Learn, but Easier to Master

.... 70

It's All in the Hips 70

   A Sore Posterior is the Sign of a Good Learning Day 70

Chapter Review: 88

Chapter 4: Planning Your Adventure! 89

Where to Go, What to Pack, and How to Do It........... 89

East Coast vs. West Coast 89

Chapter Review: 100

Chapter 5: Congrats! You've Reached the End . 101

Take What You've Learned and Apply It................... 101

About the Author 102

Recommended Resources..............................103

Chapter 1: Hey Kid, Wanna Hit the Slopes?

Gear Up!

Tailor Your Experience Like a Fine Suit

Tip 1: Learn the Difference Between Camber, Rocker, and Combo

The first and most crucial step in beginning your journey is understanding the different structures of skis and snowboards and what sets them apart. It will make you ask yourself: "What's for me? What will make me feel most comfortable?" Do we want more stability at high speeds? Do we want quick and easy turns found in a maneuverable style of riding? Or do we want as much vertical "pop" as possible when we're ripping it through a terrain park? Thankfully, the terminology forthwith applies to both sports. Learning the difference between these variants will determine what type of terrain you wish to conquer in the end. They all have unique characteristics that lend talents to the various types of snow. While some ski and snowboard brands will label things as "all-mountain" capable, there isn't a "one size fits all" for function on a mountain, whether skiing OR snowboarding. The goal is to narrow down your options as best you can to understand what will help you achieve your goals on the mountain. There are certainly some styles better suited to beginners that are recommended, but not everyone is the same. I was a skier for many years before I transitioned to snowboarding. I was on a trip with one of my best friends who'd never skied a day in his life. I figured, "well, if you're gonna be falling every time you try to get going, I might as well do the same." I was quite stubborn at the time and chose an advanced/expert level board to demo over the next five days, but after countless falls and bruising of my tailbone, I finally found my form. For me, this helped me become a stronger snowboarder all the faster because I chose a harder route; however, everyone will be different.

Tip 2: Camber

Arguably the most popular of the variants among every class of rider from beginner to expert, this styling offers what many consider to be the most stable of the types. Whether a board or a pair of skis, camber refers to the arch that lies underneath the spot where your boots attach to your bindings. Depending on the skis' size and the rider's skill level, the point of contact will be located just behind the center of the skis. For boards, it depends on the stance width of the rider, but normally you will find the center of one's foot offset from the anchor (where your bindings screw-in) by about 2-3 inches in either direction. Depending on the stiffness or flexibility of the equipment, the arch in the camber is meant to flex downward as a rider progresses through their turns. Like an F1 car, whose wheels angle inward at low speeds and progressively become perpendicular to the ground as speed increases, the flexing of the camber creates stability that determines one's "effective edge" or what I was taught as a kid as being the thing that allows you to carve through the snow with speed and control. The almost spring-like "pop" that it offers to the rider is what makes camber fun and the stability it provides. For those who seek a bit more of an adrenaline rush in the terrain parks, it offers a great chance to launch yourself off the lip of jumps. For the types like myself, camber is a preference. The best feeling on a mountain for me is pushing deep into my turns and carving hard lines down the mountain, but if you fancy yourself a powder fiend or a "park junkie" as they're playfully known, you might want to investigate the next popular variant: Rocker.

Tip 3: Rocker

A literal antithesis to everything that camber is, rocker is what I've always considered the "fun" kinds of skis and boards. Not to say that cambered equipment isn't fun, but rocker offers a much friendlier and playful experience. In some cases, people will refer to it as reverse camber, but I've heard people use both terms. It lets newer riders adjust to learning in a much more user-friendly fashion. As we know, camber has an arch in the middle, whereas rockers almost lay flat on the snow, with your boots and bindings being completely in touch with the ground. The tips in the front and rear angle upward. The reason for this has to do with the terrain preference you'll be riding should you choose rocker equipment. While they don't offer as much carving stability as camber, rockers excel in lighter, fluffier snow. Whether it's a fresh 2-inch coat of powder on top of a groomed trail or knee-deep powder in the woods, rocker's strongest attribute is giving you "float" in these types of conditions. They're also known for their maneuverability and help the rider play around with riding switch on a snowboard or backward on skis. It's meant for the more creative riders who don't seek the speed thrills as adamantly, but those who like using their imagination. Even though there isn't nearly as much "pop" with rockers, they're popular in the terrain parks for their stability in grinding on rails or boxes. It also makes it easier for the more skilled riders to enter the jump or land backward. The only real downside to his type of equipment is that carving can be difficult. You'll almost be sliding around and not in the ways you want to. That being said, the yearning for carving usually falls to more experienced riders. Still, for people like me whose self-education in the sport came from trying the most difficult things first, it can be a nice "tough love" way of getting yourself started.

Tip 4: Rocker/Camber

Now we get into an interesting variation, one that is unique. Boards and skis with a mixture of rocker AND camber are geared more towards seasoned riders who know their bodies and how they react with certain equipment. Those with more experience will likely gravitate towards these types of builds simply because they fit the preference of these riders. Rocker/camber combos will traditionally contain camber in the center with either a rocker front tip or rocker tips on both ends of the equipment. This offers a special type of riding. While it may not perform well on groomed hardpack, it's great for versatile shredding. It assists with one's float in deeper snow but makes initiating a turn far easier because of the loft provided in the front. Tail rocker serves some purpose but should be reserved for riders who feel very comfortable in their abilities. It almost makes it seem too floaty. Your turns won't feel as earned and hard-hitting, but it makes for a fun experience. When I first learned to snowboard, the very first board I ever bought was a YES 420. An oddly short, fat powder board constructed in a way known as a "twin-directional" board. To this day, it is my favorite board that I have ever ridden but what was unique about it was its rocker/camber blend. Its tail only had minor rocker, but the front tip was the special part. Its nose was so fat and wide and lifted that it offered seamless float on powder or pack. It was designed as a powder board, but it's one of those special few boards that excels on any part of the mountain. Not to mention, it was shorter than a traditional board, so it made turning even more fun and far easier. Rocker/camber is a great option amongst the equipment variants, but as was stated before, it's better reserved for the more experienced riders.

Lay of the Land

Tip 5: Determine Where You Should Ride

Now, this is the part in the guide where it will get a little bit subjective. The determination of where one should ride depends on the skill of the rider themself. Until you've had a little more experience under your belt, I'd recommend sticking to bunny slopes, and blue squares (easy and intermediate trails) on groomed resort runs until you truly feel confident in your riding abilities. That being said, once you have mastered the greens, the blues, and even the blacks (single diamonds and double—which essentially amount to expert level and beyond), you will be able to determine exactly where you want to ride. In the next couple of tips, we will discuss the differences between all the different terrains and the skills needed to master them. As I mentioned before, I kind of threw myself into the fire from the bright young age of seven, taking on what is considered to be one of the holy grails of Alpine skiing: Ajax, otherwise, and more commonly known as Aspen. Much of the time, it is confused for Snowmass, which is an entirely different mountain about 20 minutes East down the road. The point is: if you are completely new to either of these sports, DON'T choose a mountain like that. Thankfully, I attended a week-long ski school program that safely guided us despite my efforts to explore and stray from the group. Still, there were times when I did manage to find my own adventures on trails far too difficult for the literal epitome of a beginner. The fun part of deciding what type of terrain you want to ride will essentially define who you are as a rider. I've known park rats, and I've known bowl junkies, but at the end of the day, we all share that same love and bond.

Tip 6: Bunnies and Blues

The first moment you arrive at a resort, you'll almost notice an increasing grade of terrain, sometimes going left to right, sometimes the opposite, and sometimes a mixture of the two. The simple analysis here is that the steeper the trail, the higher the grade, the more difficult the run will be. The majority of mountains the average person will visit will be 99% classified by each one of these types of trails. The remainder is reserved for the best of the best, the elite. More often than not, these won't be generically marked on a map (bowls, glades, etc.). Starting on the easiest end of things is beginners' trails which are marked on the mountain as green circles, most commonly referred to as the "bunny slopes." These will be wider, flatter, and easier going trails. For inexperienced younglings and budding riders, these will offer a laid-back experience of smooth cruising. Next, we find ourselves on the blue squares, otherwise known as the intermediate trails. These can heavily vary and will likely be the bulk of the mountain or the majority of the trails available to ride. Here we will see an increase in steepness. Depending on the region of the country or mountain you're riding on, what is labeled a blue square vs. what feels like a blue square can differ heavily. In the East, you'll find anything from wide to narrow blue runs, maybe one that goes through the trees or a nice trip above the tree line, depending on the level of the snowpack. In the West, however, you'll almost always find yourself above treeline on some of the biggest, widest, and most vast trails there are to be ridden. It gives you that sense of scale and epic, endless wonder when you're carving down something the size of a dozen football fields.

Tip 7: Blacks, and the Double Whammy

Pro-tip to all my beginners out there: do NOT test your luck with a black diamond or a double black diamond until you are absolutely sure you have reached a skill level that can accommodate such difficult trails. These can be very steep, possibly filled with a seemingly never-ending minefield of moguls (which we'll talk about later), and depending on where you are, can be slippery and icy or extremely deep in powder. These expert trails are tricky, and even for someone like myself, if I don't feel rested or alert enough, I won't risk going down one. Much like the blue squares, the steepness on blacks can vary, but the bottom line is: you had better be prepared to go fast. If you're not accustomed to high speeds at this point in your experience, tight, concise, and controlled turns are your friends. One of the challenges with blacks is your line of sight. The downward curve of the slope can sometimes be a bit of an illusion. As you progress down a slope, it may appear like you're reaching an edge that you'll almost certainly fly off of, but rest assured that isn't the case. Snow can be tricky depending on the light, and sometimes the terrain doesn't always appear as it truly is. Make no mistake though if it feels like it's steep or appears as such, there's a good chance it is. Graduating to the next level, however, double blacks are among the most difficult runs to ride in the world, no matter where they are. In layman's terms, it gets even harder here. The steepness and unpredictability of the snowpack, especially in Western states, makes this the absolute most difficult groomed (or sometimes ungroomed) type of trail offered to on-the-map riders. There isn't too much to elaborate on with double blacks because, by the time you're experienced enough, that knowledge and experience will more than speak for itself.

Tip 8: Groomers

Now this right here, THIS is Mecca. This is the bread and butter that ties all riders together. This is where a lot of your fun will be had. This is where you learn, and this is where you grow. This is where you carve beautiful and enormous S-lines down a mountainside on lined and compacted snow. This is where the passion is born for most, much like myself. Even when you first start, seeing the lines drawn deep in the snowpack will inspire you as they did for me. You see them, and it feels comfortable and manageable. Referring to a trail as a groomer or a groomed trail simply means that earlier that morning or late the night before, the snowcats (which resemble what you would imagine being winterized tanks with massive treads) in a big armada of sorts, roam up and down the mountain dragging these massive patterned pads behind them. These create the lines in the snow that most people see or recognize as a groomed trail. Not only do the cats pack the snow down, making it more stable and maneuverable, but the lines created make it much easier to carve turns and navigate the mountain with precision.

Tip 9: Powder

One of the more unique types of terrain you will experience on a mountain, powder may very well be the most versatile kind of snow you ride on. With groomers, they are exactly that: groomers. No layout of that terrain will differ too vastly from the next, because they're all created the same way. With powder, there are literal levels to this. On the one hand, you might have powder that has sprinkled overnight onto some of these groomers. It could range anywhere from two inches to two whole feet. The fun part about powder is that it can be very smooth riding. It's relaxing and enjoyable while at the same time being much quieter than riding on groomed trails or something that might be icy. Something that I've seen steer beginners away from icy or groomed trails is the sound that your equipment makes when carving on it. It can be very loud and distracting, and at times depending on how abrasive the run is, it can be a little intimidating. With powder, you have a serene, beautiful, and very quiet experience. It becomes much more difficult to catch an edge. It almost offers a floating feeling or like one you'd experience while surfing. The only drawback, in my opinion, is that with powder, it may be easier to initiate a turn, but executing and maintaining control can be much more difficult if your equipment isn't wide enough or a proper rocker variant. That being said, you don't always have to worry about how good your turns are because if you do fall hard into it, it's like jumping into a massive, fluffy pillow. Just make sure all parts of your outerwear are sealed, so you don't get loads of snow shoved into your sleeves or pants.

Tip 10: Backcountry and Bowls

Here's where we stride off the normally beaten path on mountains. This is where you are more likely to find ungroomed trails that are marked as black diamonds and double black diamonds. As I said before if you have not reached a level of competency and skill that can match these steep and sometimes very unforgiving slopes, do NOT attempt. It could very likely land you in the hospital, or God forbid something far worse. Backcountry is a bit of a broad term. Some mountains have certain areas designated as backcountry and "ungroomed slopes" where you can have a bit of an adventure exploring what is out there. Typically, the backcountry is defined by heavy/deep powder, moguls formed naturally from high winds moving snow (they are essentially giant mounds to maneuver through), and runs that go through a series of tightly knit trees are otherwise known as "glades." The final form of backcountry, and arguably THE most challenging type of terrain available to the modern rider, are bowls. This is the toughest of the tough. Often, these aren't even marked by double black diamonds but are simply marked by signs that read "Experts Only." They are viciously steep, completely natural, and prone to avalanches more often than not. Now you're out there to have fun, so unless you have the skills or a trained guide with you, do not attempt these. Due to their steep nature, the speed alone is enough to fill any adrenaline junkie's heart with joy because, in reality, they are a true pleasure. One of the greatest moments I've ever experienced came the first time I built up enough courage to drop into a bowl. Interestingly enough, it also happened to be the highest skiable point in North America, nearly three miles above sea level.

Tip 11: Terrain Parks

Now we've reached the funky part of the mountain. The terrain parks are home to what people within the culture playfully call "park rats" or "park junkies," among other things. They're known within the culture as the ones in saggy clothing, which is most of the time very colorful, and their "swaggy" approach to riding. Their riding style alone is enough to differentiate them on the mountain because of the laid-back style that they present. Amidst the many boxes, rails, and jumps, you'll see a mountain culture that is completely its own, and these folks own it. While there are plenty of people who can enjoy normal parts of the mountain like groomers and the backcountry, more often than not, you'll find people who spend their entire day on the mountain at the parks. Whether a skier or a snowboarder, they'll ride down to the end of the park, and they won't even bother taking the lifts back up. They'll simply unhook themselves from their gear and walk back up to the beginning. A great example of a world-class terrain park is Buttermilk Mountain. It's located directly adjacent to Aspen Mountain and the Aspen Highlands. It has hosted the World Championship freestyle competitions and the X Games several times over. When I say some of these jumps are terrifyingly big, I truly mean it. The sheer scale of them is mind-blowing and more than intimidating. For a guy like me, they're not my thing, but if you have experience in other sports like skateboarding, surfing, wakeboarding, or pretty much anything that involves spins, flips, and grinding rails, this could be the part of the mountain best suited for you. Last but certainly not least is the famous halfpipe. Many mountains will have these, but it's always dependent on the amount of snow a mountain receives in a given season. At Buttermilk, they have one of the biggest in the world, the walls seem to rise endlessly, and the mere thought of dropping in is frightening for someone who isn't looking to get big air and hang time. Similar to the backcountry and bowls, don't venture in here unless you have the experience because not only will you hurt yourself pretty badly, but you'll likely be verbally berated by any onlookers.

Tip 12: Avalanches

Perhaps the scariest thing one can experience on a mountain short of botching a big air jump or catching an edge and tumbling down a steep slope, avalanches are the result of unstable layers of snow becoming loose and sliding down a mountain. Picture the top layer of an onion sliding off and revealing the smoother, denser inside; only when it slides off, it's less abrasive than the tough exterior of an onion, more like smoked brisket falling right off the bone. Once that top layer begins to break away, it will build and cascade, growing larger in speed and size. The higher up one starts, the deadlier it can become. They can reach speeds of over 100 miles per hour and can wipe out everything in their path. Trees, buildings, and most frighteningly of all: people. If you ever find yourself caught in an avalanche, there are two things to keep in mind. If one starts above you (behind you), stop traveling vertically, and begin riding horizontally as fast as you can. If you can get out of its path, you will more than likely be in a good position. If you find yourself in the shifting snowpack, do your best to remain calm but know that it is a terrifying experience. It is best to act like you are swimming, actively circulating your arms; this will be your best chance at not falling beneath the wave of snow. The reassuring thing is that avalanches are mostly secluded to the western states, like places in the Rockies, Northern California, and some of the more secluded mountains in Utah, Idaho, and Wyoming. Another reassurance is that all of these places take extreme precautionary measures to ensure that people don't cause or get caught in these hellacious natural disasters. After new snowfall, mountain crews will use explosives to create controlled explosions that will offset new and heavy snowfall to ensure that they can't happen with people on the slopes. Surprisingly, it doesn't take much to create an avalanche. At higher altitudes, in the thinner air, even a loud shout can echo and reverberate to shift the top layer of snow. Even the physical actions of one rider hitting the wrong angle at the wrong time can shift the snow. But with modern technology, most have little to worry about, even though it is always smart to stay vigilant on the mountain.

Reasons Behind the Recs

Tip 13: Why YOU Should Plan a Trip to Breckenridge, CO (Part I)

At the tender age of 21, in 2016, some of my best friends and I decided that we should take a trip to Colorado in our Junior Year of college (Senior Year for two of our friends). We meticulously planned this excursion for months before finally deciding what mountain to venture to. After due consideration, we figured "go big, or go home," and with that: "Breck," as we came to call it, was the long-sought-after destination. My friends and I went to school in Fort Worth, Texas, so a relatively easy 15-hour drive was all that stood in our way of some of the prettiest slopes in the world. After a red-eye wake-up, our road trip adventure consumed an entire day, but upon arriving at the house, we had reserved, we quickly unloaded, took a load off, and prepared for the day ahead. The first day we were lucky to hit the slopes in possibly one of the biggest blizzards I have ever witnessed in my life. Visibility reached maybe 50 yards at max, but it was magical. There was about a foot of fresh powder laced over the beautiful, expansive blue squares we were taking on. A warm-up day is good, seeing that we didn't want to push ourselves too hard too fast. Since I am a skier and a snowboarder, I found this to be the perfect opportunity to try out my new board: a twin directional powder board with a center camber and a rocker front tip. Dubbed the 420 by YES, a Switzerland-based company, this board hit the market hot and redefined what a snowboard could do. Relatively short for someone my height (six foot even), this board measured roughly 154 centimeters in length, but the length and maneuverability weren't the highlights; the width was. Easily the fattest board I have ever owned or ridden, with my toes and heels being nowhere near the edge of the board, it was the perfect tool for an otherwise perfect powder day.

Tip 14: Why YOU Should Plan a Trip to Breckenridge, CO (Part II)

After the second day of continuous snow, the fresh powder began to subside as it gave way to droves of people constantly breaking it up. Once it had, the days opened up into beautiful sunny clear blue skies. We decided to take a day to rest since we would be there for a full week. We had the chance to explore the town and even celebrate my good friend's 21st birthday. Not nearly enough can be said about how beautiful of a village Breckenridge has. A really fun aspect of major mountains like these is the adorable village centers that sit at their base. Flush with shops and amazing restaurants, all within very close proximity to the apartment we'd rented, we had managed to find lots to do as a group. All in all, it felt cozy and homey even though it was a place none of us had ever been before. However, the next day, I would soon come to recognize as one of the greatest in all my life.

Tip 15: Why YOU Should Plan a Trip to Breckenridge, CO (Part III)

Today was the day, perhaps 80% of the reason we chose Breck over all the other major mountains along the "Mountain Highway" or the several hundred mile stretch of ski slope laced road that runs through the entire western half of Colorado on the way to Denver (which includes but is not limited to Aspen, Vail, Copper Mountain, Keystone, and Arapahoe Basin). We chose Breck because not only does it possess beautiful snowcapped vistas and vast open trails, but the highest ski lift in North America. The ski lift itself climbs to approximately 12,840 feet, and once there, you can decide if you would like to ski down from there, down a fairly steep slope, or climb even further, up to the highest skiable point in all of North America. The only other places like this on the continent are accessible by helicopter or a grueling hike. We were about to undertake a grueling hike of our own. While only 160 vertical feet, it was roughly 300 diagonal feet up the final stretch to reach the summit of the Imperial Bowl: a whopping 13,001 feet above sea level. Despite being in fairly good shape at the time, this was by and far the most difficult physical task I have ever attempted in my entire life. The air at that altitude is so thin that anyone not used to it is going to have a hard time breathing. Pro tip: I would not recommend such a thing to anyone with asthma without a pressurized oxygen mask because you will more than likely pass out. As my friend and I began our ascension, I immediately began breathing very heavily. We'll come to learn later in this guide, but ski boots are NOT fun to walk in (it was later in the day, and in the spring, the snow will melt a little and become heavier, so I opted for skiing down this instead of snowboarding). They are thick, dense, and rock-solid boots that are difficult enough to walk in, let alone hiking up a bare mountainside. I was taking my time but moving as fast as I could so as not to hold up the line of people behind me. Even that wasn't enough because two men seemingly in their mid to late 60s ended up overtaking me. It was a little embarrassing, but I took it on the chin and with some humility. After a solid 30 minutes of truly brutal exhaustion, we reached the top, and as expected: I collapsed and passed out.

Tip 16: Why YOU Should Plan a Trip to Breckenridge, CO (Part IV)

So, I don't really remember passing out, but when I did come to, I woke up to my friend and a Ski Patrolman standing over me, checking on me and trying to give me water. After about five or so minutes of catching my breath and hydrating, I finally sat up and was able to see exactly what was around me. It was a very euphoric and almost inexplicable feeling. I had reached one of the highest peaks on earth; what I saw before me was breathtaking. Instantly at that moment, I was reminded of a quote from one of my favorite movies. The words played in my head like a recorded track: "When Alexander saw the breadth of his domain, he wept, for there were no more worlds left to conquer." And at that moment, I did, in fact, cry. It was the most beautiful thing I had ever seen in my life. Witnessing the world from 13,000 feet in one of the most stunning mountain ranges known to man, I was overcome with emotion. Although I have explored many a mountain since then, to this day, there has been no view, sight, or feeling I have had that has ever matched that. After some time, walking around the top of the peak, taking some photos, and looking east towards a series of extra bowls and narrow chutes too difficult even for someone as experienced as me, I began to mentally prepare myself for the inexplicably steep slope I was about to drop into. I had some more water, selected the perfect song, and locked into my skis. I dropped my goggles down and slowly inched towards the edge. My skis were about halfway over when I fully grasped just how STEEP this bowl was. For a good 20-30 feet below me, it was a literal straight drop, but at that moment, I had the greatest surge of adrenaline I had ever felt, and I took hold of it. What followed was the single greatest run of my life. I felt like a man possessed. I was FLYING down this slope. Everything I had ever learned had brought me to this moment to take complete advantage of it. We reached the bottom of the mountain to go have lunch. My friend and I didn't say a word to each other until we were about two beers in simply because of the shock and awe we had experienced. Truly one of the best moments of my life.

Tip 17: Why YOU Should Try Equipment That (Literally) Fits You

This one is pretty simple. When it comes to snowboards or skis, the standard measuring stick is your own body. Typically, a board or pair of skis should reach just below the top of your head by about two inches, so for someone like me who is six foot even, a recommended ski length would be between 170-190 centimeters. Through the years, I have owned skis that have been shorter and taller than me, and the same applies to boards. You would see me riding a board in similar length, if not slightly shorter. Another factor that comes into play is someone's weight in direct relation to their height, so for someone like me who is also fairly heavy, I would need a few extra centimeters in length and also wider equipment. Tread softly with equipment width though, because the wider the skis or board, the more advanced the equipment is— meaning it is reserved for more skilled riders.

Tip 18: Equipment Rental

Every rider, young and old, no matter when or where they begin their mountain journeys, is going to start here. Renting equipment is the easiest way to try new skis and boards that you otherwise may not have had access to. It is something I highly recommend to anyone wanting to get started. Depending on the resort you are visiting or inventory they may possess, you will either have to rent low-quality equipment or seek more expensive ways to try out equipment. In my opinion, there are only two real drawbacks to renting equipment (especially if it is constantly). The first of which is the cost. Nothing about these sports ever really comes cheap, but if you are getting 30-40 days on a mountain in season, you will be spending a LOT of money, so it's wise to find what fits you best and eventually make a purchase decision. Secondly is the quality of this equipment. In my own experience, nine out of ten times, rental equipment is old, beaten down from constant use, and never quite what you're hoping it will be. It can be convenient when you are given a package combo rental of boots, skis, and poles (which can sometimes be a good bargain), but these things will be at least five or more years old—the same applies for boards. Much like golf, don't buy the farm if you're not serious about taking on these sports. Regardless of the quality or short-term costs, try renting for a time until you build up your skills. Renting can also be useful if you don't want to commit to buying skis or a board yet. Many people like myself (for many years before committing) had purchased boots for each sport and would rent or demo different skis and boards to find what I liked (which is why boots should always be the first thing you purchase, but we'll discuss that later). Pro tip: it also makes travel much easier when you're going far for your mountain destination. Closing thoughts on renting: if you're teaching a toddler to ride, rent them boots until they've stopped growing. You will save thousands of dollars.

Tip 19: Equipment Demo

The biggest difference between renting and demoing equipment (aside from an occasional small price difference) is the far superior quality that demo equipment provides. Now, you can demo boots and bindings in some very niche places, but demoing sticks mainly to skis and boards more often than not. What makes this so fun is that you are getting brand new, top-of-the-line products for that season when you're demoing vs. renting. I've done it several times in my life, and it has led me to know what products I want to buy and don't want to buy. For example, while on that aforementioned trip to Breck, I demoed a set of skis from the company Blizzard, known as the Brahmas. These were an exceptional pair of all-mountain, true-twin skis that allowed for float but also carving abilities since they were a rocker-camber combination. Although I loved them, and they took me down the infamous Imperial Bowl, I learned that these weren't necessarily my fit. I realized I needed something just a bit wider for my size (regardless of how brilliant these skis were). In time (after a demo at Mammoth Mountain in northern California), I discovered that the Candide Thovex Faction 2.0's was more my speed (aptly named for the highly revered French off-piste skier) because of how wide they are and the lift they provide on lighter snowpack. The reason I'd recommend demoing (mainly when you already have your own boots) is that you will get a more accurate understanding of the type of product you're testing and the type of product you will eventually need if you're serious about committing to learning these sports. Renting old and broken-in gear will certainly be easier, but in the long run, it isn't going to benefit you like demoing will. However, if you are bold, you may jump straight to buying if you want the most cost-effective long-term option.

Tip 20: BYOB (Bring Your Own Boots)

Now, we have reached the portion of this where we'll discuss the final part of the equipment journey. It will be a long series of trials and errors to narrow down what equipment you will eventually spend thousands of dollars on. Much like a custom-fitted set of golf clubs, the long-term investment of buying your own boots, bindings, and board/skis should last you at the very least five to six years. You want it to fit you properly; you want it to serve your interests because, as I said, the massive amount of money you will spend on this will directly affect your experiences on the mountain. While I have talked about renting and demoing your equipment to find the perfect fit, I briefly mentioned boots being the first key investment in your equipment. Once you understand your body and how it reacts to certain equipment, you will find that the most important piece you can buy, what starts it all: is your boots. The first thing you should invest in purchasing once you know yourself as a rider is your boots. This is key for several reasons. Once you possess your own pair of boots, but not yet skis or a board, it can make travel extremely easy. I am someone who has flown across the country with my massive bag containing my skis and my board; it's taller than I am! It can be such a hassle to transport something like that, not to mention being fairly pricey. However, if all you have is a boot bag to take with you, all you'll need is a rental or demo once you arrive at your destination. It allows a little more freedom in trying out different skis and boards because, after enough time, your boots will be worn in and properly fit your feet, allowing you to have the most comfortable and beneficial experience moving forward with your selection.

Tip 21: What Past Athletic Experience Can Do for You

More commonly than not, people who have had some experience in other sports whose skills can translate to a mountain may tend to seek out a snowier experience. Skateboarders and surfers usually find that snowboarding comes very naturally to them, whereas people who rollerblade or ice skate find skiing to come very naturally as well. For me, this was never the case since I started so young, I had never had experience in other sports like those, but on my ski trip to Breckenridge, I had the pleasure of teaching my good friend how to snowboard. He had some experience in skateboarding but, more importantly, many years of experience as a surfer. This transitioned beautifully to the slopes, seeing that he had already worked his way up to the intermediate blue squares within the first couple hours of our first day on the mountain. It was amazing to see! So, while it isn't the most important aspect of learning how to ride, it can certainly be helpful for those who have had minor or even extensive experience in these areas. I will say it does pertain a bit more to people seeking to snowboard. Still, going from two sports like skating and surfing, transitioning from sports where your feet are not secured to the board they're riding, having the security of being strapped in allows them to feel more comfortable much more quickly.

Brand Recommendations

Tip 22: Choosing the Right Brands

Within this section, herein lies my personal recommendations for the brands that I feel are suitable for beginners and experts alike for skiing and snowboarding. These are recommendations I'll be making through my years of experience. Even after all that I have been through with these mountain sports, it still took me years to make purchases that I still use to this day. Were it not for the countless times renting and demoing different skis, boards, and boots for both sports, I would not have arrived at the conclusions I did. Keep in mind that all of the major, as well as independent brands, do have options for beginners, intermediates, and experts. Still, I will share my experiences and thoughts on what I would recommend for riders of all experience levels. Keep in mind while these are my opinions that I stand by and have formed through my years of experience, I still recommend using your own experiences as the baseline test for where you will go in your journey.

Tip 23: Ski Brands for Beginners

As I have said before, all brands will offer wide ranges of skis that adhere to all skill levels, but some in my experience that are great for beginners are K2, Solomon, and Rossignol. K2 is one of the most widely regarded and recognizable brands in the world. More often than not, this is one of the dominant brands you will see at resorts that are available for rental. They are deeply rooted in race skiing and their known abilities in camber profiling. They are meant to carve and hold their edges and offer greater stability which is very helpful to new riders. Excellent for groomers. Next, we have Solomon. Their beginner skis are a tad more playful. You will find options in directional tips and twin tips (which can typically be camber/rocker variants. These skis will be directed towards all parts of the mountain. Whether groomers or powder, they will perform adequately. They were the first brand I ever rented when I was only seven years old in Aspen, Colorado. They served me well and allowed me to enjoy my experience and spark a lifelong passion. Finally, we have the first brand that I ever committed to purchasing: Rossignol. This pair was a wonderfully lively pair of twin tips with a rocker/camber combo. They were so much fun to grow up with, and I managed to have eight years of experience with them until I eventually outgrew them. I got them at the age of twelve, and they served me well through many ski trips. Rossignol, or "Rossis," as many refer to them, really specialize in youth skis as well. It's a brand I'd highly recommend for parents looking to inspire their toddlers or young kids to try the sport. On average, beginner skis like these will run anywhere from $300-500 brand new. They tend to be on the lower end of stiffness, offering a great deal of flexibility.

Tip 24: Ski Brands for Intermediates

While it can be difficult to completely categorize a distinct difference between intermediate and expert, they are pretty enveloping terms. Intermediate skis will make up a majority of the available market, while expert skis are very select. There aren't as many that are solely labeled for "experts" because so many of the intermediate variety will be compounded as expert skis as well. My first two brand examples will be companies that I feel offer a great range of intermediate skis, while the third and final one is one I consider an excellent expert company and the skis that I currently ride on. The first brand is Blizzard. I mentioned earlier that these were the first skis that I ever demoed. The model in question was the Blizzard Bonafide. This was my first experience with particularly large skis. They're long, wide, and quite fast. They very much adhere to my particular style of riding (which I apply to skiing and snowboarding), known commonly as "charging." These are meant for the big mountains, the big trails, and massive off-piste, Alpine riding. The float they create is tough and precise, but they allow you to carve out these amazing, beautiful turns. Although I didn't end up purchasing them after my four-day demo in Breckenridge, it is a brand and particular model I would recommend to anyone whose skill has reached a level where they can handle such equipment. The second intermediate (to expert) brand I would recommend is Nordica, specifically their Enforcer model. These are the skis I demoed on my trip to Aspen/Snowmass, Colorado. Although these were a tad narrower than the skis I own now and something I would prefer, these proved to be extremely fun. With a lightweight carbon fiber design, these skis showed their insane versatility. Even though they were larger than what would be recommended for someone my height, beginning a turn in them was shockingly easy. They were stable at high speeds and performed well on groomers and in powder. Skis of these varieties will range from $500-700 brand new (approximately). These tend to be in the mid-high-end flexibility range, remaining somewhat playful but also more serious than beginner skis.

Tip 25: Ski Brand for Experts

We have now arrived at what I consider to be an undeniably elite and top-tier brand: Faction. This is the brand of ski that I currently ride on and have been for roughly three years now. These are the longest, widest, and certainly the most difficult skis I have ever had the pleasure of hitting the slopes with. The model in question that I own is the Candide Thovex 2.0. These are probably the most storied and popular models in Faction's lineup. Their notoriety and fame come from the person they are named after, Candide Thovex. This French alpine skier became famous through a series of YouTube videos several years back of him ripping through the French Alps, pulling off all kinds of insane stunts: single and double backflips, jumping over people, going through ice caves and chutes. It was a massive inspiration for me. Even though I knew that I would never be able to achieve those types of maneuvers, I wanted to know more about him. I soon discovered that he did, in fact, have skis named after him, and not only that: he had helped to design them as well. Faction isn't the best-known ski company, and there are few people out there aside from the passionate and obsessed types like myself. They were made for riders like Candide. Those who love the big wide-open spaces that typically tend to be natural slopes, ungroomed and unedited. They're fat and floaty for the natural powder but hard and sharp for the groomed trails. In my experience, they do perform well on all parts of the mountain. With all that being said, these are not easy skis to ride. The learning curve I experienced was massive and, quite frankly, humbling. I hadn't rented, demoed, or even seen these in person before I unboxed them on Christmas morning (thank you, by the way, Mom). Faction is an outstanding brand to try and truly a cut above the rest for those with the skills that kill. Very rigid and stiff, this brand will keep you on your toes (literally). Their lineup and other expert-level skis will likely land somewhere between $700 up to over $1000 in some brands. My specific pair was around $800.

Tip 26: Choosing the Right Brands (Understanding the Culture)

Ski brands of all varieties and niches, no matter how broad, like K2, or how minuscule, like Faction; every company will have that wide range of equipment that stretches across all skill levels, no matter what. Such is life with the snowboarding world. Keep in mind the cultures of skiing and snowboarding could not be any different than they are. Skiing has always been viewed and revered with such poise, especially with its extensive history in the Winter Olympics. It had class, and it had that edge; it was so deeply rooted in history and respect. Here comes this wild man's sport riding a big fat board down the slopes. It became the skating and surfing of the snowcapped mountains. Those cultures almost collided and found themselves on a whole new playing field. It was a revolution of swagger, style, and a fun, easygoing sport. Recreational resort skiing has been around for the better part of a century, whereas snowboarding only made its debut in popularity in the early '80s. Towards the end of the '70s, Jake Burton came out of nowhere with a design that changed mountain sports forever. People thought this guy was crazy because he had managed to attach two feet to the same piece of wood. Not long after, he founded Burton snowboards, which is where our journey begins.

Tip 27: Snowboard Brands for Beginners

Burton! Inarguably THE single biggest name in the snowboarding world. Why? Because this is where it all began. For over four decades, Burton has remained the pinnacle of snowboarding culture and its followers. It is very difficult to visit any major or minor mountain resort without seeing a Burton board at least once. If you're planning on renting generic equipment at a mountain nine out of ten times, it's going to be Burton. There are reasons for that: it's reliable, great to learn on, and seemingly lasts forever. My journey in learning how to (or rather teaching myself how to) snowboard actually began on a Burton board. Once upon a time, I brought a good friend to my home mountain of Shawnee Peak in Bridgton, Maine, to teach him how to ski. Without being too harsh...it was pretty brutal. So, after a day of slowly easing down the mountain while he fell, I figured, hey, I might as well do the same. After five days of falling on my butt, I eventually got it down and was able to start my new passion in boarding, to add to my already polished experience in skiing. Burton is an outstanding place to start for beginners. While they do have a mind-blowingly big range of boards from beginner to expert, their lower-end models will suit newcomers young and old. Although K2 is predominantly known for its skis, it also has a big following for the boards it produces. While it may not be the first choice amongst seasoned riders, it nonetheless provides a great catalog for those starting off. Finally, we have Never Summer. This was the first board company I ever demoed (vs. rented), and even though I was a budding boarder, it did not disappoint. It was a nice way to find out that a lopsided board wasn't necessarily for me. The odd design of this particular model had an odd nose and tail, tapering almost like a trapezoid. Their lower-end/beginner models may be a bit stiffer than other entry-level brands, but still a really fun brand in my experience. Prices for these types of boards will be similar to beginner skis, and the same will apply for each skill level of boards forthwith.

Tip 28: Snowboard Brands for Intermediates

First, we have Lib Tech. A relatively new company in the snowboarding scene, they've gained serious popularity in the last decade due to their wide range of appeal. They're really meant to be a "one size fits all" type of mountain board. Do you want groomers? Check. Do you want to hit the terrain parks? You're covered. Desire to float carelessly over knee-deep powder? It can be done. This brand has been praised for its delicately high-tech boards that can carve just as efficiently as they can surf. They've been made particularly famous in the last decade by a man widely regarded as the best snowboarder in the world: Travis Rice. A man who became a real inspiration for me when I first started, Rice burst onto the global scene at the tender age of seventeen when he launched himself over a 120-foot gap at Mammoth Mountain. He has since been the leading influence in big mountain riding. This man has pushed the limits of riding further than anyone has ever dared. His models within the Lib Tech lineup are outstanding and truly fitting for seasoned riders who would hesitate to call them experts; however, some models would be fitting for someone of similar talent to Travis himself. Second, we have YES. Now, this is a unique brand. Nowhere near the fame or popularity of previously mentioned brands, YES is more of a boutique brand that adheres to very specific aspects of riding. One of the things that they truly excel in is powder boards and the first board I ever committed to purchasing: the legendary, the always reliable, the mind-blowing 420. I remember, so distinctly, reading the website when I wanted to order it. "This board will change how you think about snowboarding." I knew I had to have it from that moment, and it did not disappoint. Riding on a board, so fat that your heels and toes are nowhere near the edge, gave a never-before-experienced feeling of float. It initiated turns like no other board I'd ever felt. The front end had such rocker lift that any powder runs were yours for the conquering; it almost gave the feeling of flying. Then as now, I have never seen such a wide board. What made it even more fun was how untraditionally short the board was. It was very agile and forgiving. Sadly, on a trip to Aspen, I was getting too goofy with my riding down a flat trail and cracked the board. She now resides in the great terrain park in the sky but was an overly joyful board to own.

Tip 29: Snowboard Brands for Experts

Much like my final brand recommendation for skis, this expert snowboard brand is the one I just so happen to be riding currently. This brand comes from a man whose lifelong journey has been defined by freeriding (backcountry exploration). A family man, husband, and father whose brand truly feels like it has that wholesome, familial nature to it. Of course, I am talking about Jones Snowboards, created by the one and only Jeremy Jones. Although it is the newest brand mentioned here, it has had such a meaningful impact on the snowboarding world. Early on, the concept of snowboarding was so closely related to surfing and the mindset of "floating" and gliding over the top of thick, luscious powder. While these boards can do that, they are defined by their adhering to hard-charging, and carving has become their defining trait. Before receiving this board, I only thought I knew what it meant to carve. Sure, I had come to understand that with skiing, but my experience with snowboarding up to that point in no way could have prepared me for this. Crafted with the utmost precision, the beautiful wood grain top is what you see as you look down at the passing slopes, cutting effortlessly down groomers and beyond. For someone like me, charging is my preferred style of riding. Since I'm a larger breed, it isn't difficult for me to gain momentum when racing downhill, but I use it to my advantage. The stiffness of my board, the Flagship (the literal flagship of Jones' five board men's lineup), allows me to cut the deepest lines with unmatched stability and control. It truly is a marvel of board innovation and a beautiful sight to behold. I have never been able to get my body so close to the mountain before. It's no exaggeration. When carving a big beautiful S-line on a grand groomer, my chest at times has come within six inches of the snowpack. It is the ultimate feeling of freedom, and for me, there is nothing that can beat that. The rigidity of these boards alone sets it apart into the expert category, but I would suggest it for anyone who has reached this skill level. It is extremely hard to find something better than this, in my opinion.

Tip 30: In Conclusion...

In this life of icy ridges and windswept snowpack, everyone's journey is going to play out differently. Much like a weight loss journey, *everyone* will have a unique experience that will fit them. You can't get it so wrong that it eventually becomes right; you will simply find what fits you best. There is a lot of trial and error. You may have financial regrets in some instances (I certainly know I have), but in time and with experience, you will discover what is best for YOU. Even now, I have plenty of qualms with the equipment I own, but the pros do outweigh the cons for me. Once you have come to understand your body, your riding style, and the types of skis or boards that work best for you, you will have experiences and memories to last you a lifetime. Achieving that clarity will make your life on the mountain all the more enjoyable. Keep in mind that these recommendations have worked for ME, and I encourage everyone to find their own way but still believe in the brands I've spoken of. With that in mind, best of luck, remember patience, and above all, enjoy yourself.

One Last Story

Tip 31: Why YOU Should Plan a Trip to Aspen, CO (Part I)

No less than a year after my college excursion to the winter wonderland of Breckenridge, my friends and I were already planning our next Spring Break excursion for our final year of college. Unlike many of our counterparts, we weren't interested in some beach in Mexico where the only objective was to drink to our heart's content; we wanted more adventure. To go even further into the endless dreamy landscapes that Colorado has to offer. To quote one of my favorite comedies: "Someplace warm, a place where the beer flows like wine, where beautiful women flock like the salmon of Capistrano. I'm talking about a little place called...Aspen." Thanks to a newfound friend of ours, we actually didn't have to rent a place to stay, but rather a beautiful mansion about a five-minute drive from Snowmass. While four of my friends decided to fly there, the other four of us decided, "Hey! Why not? Let's road trip," and so we did. Departing at the brisk and pitch-black hour of 3:30 AM, we set out from Fort Worth, Texas. Since I don't mind driving, nor do I mind long stretches of driving, I was comfortable letting my friends sleep while I drove us. The northwest passage of Texas up to Colorado is an interesting drive. There's about an eighty-mile stretch of desert back roads up past Amarillo, and let me tell you, when the only light you have are your high beams and a full moon, it is slightly terrifying, but nonetheless, I pressed on. It's almost beautiful despite how creepy it can be. A short fourteen hours went by, and sooner than we knew it, we had arrived. We were greeted by our other friends who had beat us there, and we got to soak in not only this gorgeous mansion that was our home for the next week but the immense and majestic surroundings that we became witnesses to. After a few beers and some delicious pizza, we nestled in for the evening, ready to take on the mountain, and the impending blizzard, the following day.

Tip 32: Why YOU Should Plan a Trip to Aspen, CO (Part II)

There's a common misconception about Aspen: it is actually made up of four different mountains. Most people hear "Aspen" and think that's the end of it. Thankfully for those seeking adventure, that simply isn't the case. We were staying nearby Snowmass, which is the biggest and most family-friendly of the mountains. It has the most acreage and the biggest number of trails accommodating all skill levels. This is where we spent most of our time, but about fifteen minutes down the road is where we find the rest. While

Snowmass is a fun, cute little village with an equally cute and easygoing mountain (for the most part), Aspen and its surrounding peaks crank up the volume in a sense. The town of Aspen itself is reserved for the skiing elite. Think Beverly Hills in a mountain landscape. Homes here price in the high tens of millions, and the shops and restaurants are sure to put a massive dent in your bank account as well. Nonetheless, there are still places for the casual traveler to enjoy, but make no mistake, this is not for the casual rider. First, we have Aspen Mountain, most commonly referred to as "Ajax," while it has offerings for intermediate riders, don't be fooled; this is a difficult mountain. The day we were there, we watched the world qualifiers for downhill racing for the Winter Olympics, and it was a sight to behold. Not only was the course immensely steep, but just off to the side, on a huge face being ridden by recreational riders, was easily the biggest minefield of moguls I have ever seen in my life. It was scary. As someone who prefers charging groomers, something like that is quite intimidating. It was one of those "beautiful yet terrifying" sights to even someone as experienced as me.

Tip 33: Why YOU Should Plan a Trip to Aspen, CO (Part III)

Next, we have Buttermilk. This is a fun one. In one part, you have some of the biggest and most beautiful groomers west of the Mississippi, and on the other part, you have one of the biggest and most export-oriented terrain parks in the world. Nearly every year, it has hosted the Winter X-Games for the last twenty years. The jumps here are as big as medium-sized houses; I mean, it is truly amazing. Aside from that, Buttermilk is a very family-friendly mountain. It makes you feel at home and comfortable, and the parts for kids are a really terrific learning ground. The third mountain is what is known as the Aspen Highlands. Unlike Buttermilk and its versatility, this is an expert's playground. Full of ungroomed and off-piste riding, these are where the bowls and chutes lay. While you can ride the lifts up, a popular option in this neck of the woods is hiking to the tops of different summits. In the culture, this is what is known as "earning your turns" and a method that predates even the earliest ski lifts. It's the most natural and spiritual thing one can experience on a mountain. I'll admit, I've only done this once in my life (outside of my Breckenridge summit), and let me tell you, it isn't for the faint of hard; it's hard. Trudging through deep snow in stiff boots gets your heart pumping, especially when it's up a particularly large mountain face. Nonetheless, this remains such a genuine initiation into the purest form of appreciating and respecting the mountain. The Highlands is full of experiences like this, and it's something I would suggest to anyone who has achieved the skill level for it. You'll thank me when you see how amazing the views are too.

Tip 34: Why YOU Should Plan a Trip to Aspen, CO (Part IV)

Finally, we have Snowmass. This is the BIG resort. There are quite literally hundreds of trails to explore and wander through. You have your easy greens, fun blues, challenging blacks, scary double blacks, and more. There are a large handful of really fun runs through beautifully spaced glades as well. Some of my favorites are the blue square groomers that span over most of the mountain. The fun part about it is that a great deal of these blue squares lay above the tree line, which sounds weird, but the first time you experience it, it's almost comparable to flight. It can be slightly intimidating, but my goodness, is it freeing; and as you look out, far beyond the reaches of the vast mountain peaks, past the lifts and the trees, you feel at peace. There is nothing but *you* and all that lay before you. You'll find yourself soaring at breakneck speeds, not thinking about anything but the next turn you'll carve deep into the snow. To me, there is nothing more magical than that. This is where my journey began, where a passion was born, and where a simple few days in a far-off place changed my life forever. I hope, implore, and encourage every rider, young and old, new and seasoned, to visit this beautiful and mystical winter wonderland.

The Foundation on Top of the Foundation

If the Boot Fits, It Also Binds

Tip 35: Lock In!

The next step in your process will be seeking out and selecting what bindings you want. This is an important part of your journey, seeing that these are the middle ground between the boots and the equipment you're riding. It is the piece of plastic and metal bolted to your skis or board and, in turn, what you lock your boots into before you venture down a slope. In my opinion, the selection of bindings isn't as crucial as what you choose to ride or the boots you choose to wear, but a crucial step nonetheless. Bindings will be categorized by size. Narrower bindings will fit smaller boots for children or smaller footed adults and will increase in breadth the larger your equipment. The bindings I have on my skis and board are quite large, and even then, my XL snowboard bindings don't fit my boots as well as they should. My best advice to anyone with sizing concerns is to speak to whatever pro is working at a ski shop to help you fit your boots to the proper bindings. It isn't as much of a concern for skis since the fashion in which they snap in feels exceedingly different from how your snowboard boots strap into their respective bindings.

Tip 36: Ski Bindings

Ski bindings are comprised of two separate pieces locked into separate parts of each ski. The method of locking yourself into them involves inserting the toe of your boot in first and then forcefully pressing your heel down until you hear a snap. Once you hear the snap, you'll see the tail pop up to be in a near-vertical positioning. This is what you'll use to snap out of your bindings at the end of a run or when you're heading into the lodge for a mid-day lunch break. Simply lift your other foot over the top of it to press down. Certainly, a faster and easier way of detaching yourself than snowboarding. As is the same with skis and boards (and you'll soon come to find with boots), bindings have a spectrum of flexibility. Beginner bindings will have much more give and be more forgiving when initiating a turn, whereas the more you increase the skill level of the equipment, the tighter and more rigid the bindings will be. Once you've graduated to those expert-level bindings, your body will presumably have gotten stronger through experience, meaning the stiff nature of the bindings will help your turns to be even more precise. Unlike skis and boots (in my experience), the prices of bindings usually directly correlate with their quality. I purchased the first ski bindings with a little over $100, and after maybe two weeks' worth of mountain days, both had cracked. Sometime after that, I purchased a set of bindings worth around $300, and they've served me well over the last seven years. Something similar occurred with my first snowboard bindings. My advice: if you want it to last, put the money down for it.

Tip 37: Snowboard Bindings

The difference between these and ski bindings couldn't be more blatantly opposite. Where ski bindings find you locking yourself into a system that "snaps" you into place, snowboard bindings will find you "placing" your boots into their cradle and strapping your feet tightly into them. You slide your heel down the backing until your foot lays flat across the base. Once it's secured within the walls, you'll secure your toe strap across the breadth of the tip of your boot, so it pushes it back up against the wall properly. Finally, you will secure the top strap to fully secure yourself. Perhaps one of the most noticeable differences between the two sports is getting on and off the ski lift. With skiing, you stay attached to your skis for the majority of the day. You click in, enter the ski lift, exit, ride down…and then repeat. With snowboarding, you'll unlatch your back foot at the end of a run for the sake of controlling yourself as you inch through the lift line to ride it back up to the top. Small detail, but worth mentioning. As I said, with ski bindings, snowboard binding's stiffness affects their ride capabilities. In my own experience, I've found the stiffness of board bindings to play a more crucial part in your riding than ski bindings do. When you narrow down its logic, the force you apply to snowboard bindings in your turns feels more important than that of skis. In skiing, the pressure applied focuses more on your edges than the pressure you put on your bindings.

Tip 38: Poles

While this is a small detour, it's an important piece of equipment to mention. When you first learn how to ski, ten out of ten times, you will learn to ski without poles. The reason behind this lies in finding your ability to balance on your own, without knowing that the poles are there to mark your turns as you make them. They're also tremendously helpful on flatter trails where you may find yourself slowing to a halt after losing your momentum; they make it very easy to push yourself along in cadence with the pushing-off of your feet. Your stability will become muscle memory as you become more comfortable in your abilities. The poles remain as a way to keep your arms out, effectively acting as a mental barrier for your balance. They also do add a layer of swagger to your ski style. The length of your poles is usually meant to stand at a height that sits just above your waist. While gripping them, your arms should rest at a ninety-degree angle, with your forearms perpendicular to the ground. Many skiers don't adhere to that these days and tend to prefer shorter poles. I find myself in a similar category.

Tip 39: Ski Boots

Ahh yes, we have arrived here: the most uncomfortable piece of footwear you'll ever wear (at first). Ski boots are easily discernable by their extremely tough exterior. I mean, this thing could stop a bullet (don't try it), but that's certainly what it feels like. The plastic these boots are made of is so dense that I've actually used the tips to kick away ice from certain surfaces. Fret not, though; the inside is filled with very comfortable and moldable lining. Make no mistake, it does take a handful of hard riding days on the mountain to fully break them in, but once they are, it's very warm and cozy; it gives you a lot of freedom to have an experience on the mountain that is very forgiving on your feet (trust me they'll be very sore). For the first two weeks of riding, I highly recommend thicker socks, not just for the warmth, but to make sure you don't develop any nasty blisters (it will completely ruin your day). Much like bindings and the gear you ride on, boots have a stiffness spectrum depending on your level of skill (noticing the redundancy here?). So, as I've mentioned before, try out a couple of different boots, whether demo or rental, find the brands that work best for you. My advice to parents teaching their younglings is to please wait until they've fully grown before you commit to buying them boots because the frustration and money spent on new boots over the years will add up. Having said that, if you are fully grown and somewhat late to this party, make boots your first investment. They'll last you longer than anything else in your mountain arsenal. Not to mention, you'll build a level of comfort and trust with them through the years. Spend more on boots in the beginning, you'll want the quality, and the long-term investment will be beneficial. They're also the equipment that is least likely to wear down. Ski boots don't differ too much from one model to the next and have remained the same for the most part. There are three to four metal latches up and down the toes and calve, with varying levels of tightness. Occasionally, there will be a Velcro strap at the very top of the boot to create extra stability for your leg.

Tip 40: Snowboard Boots

Take a deep breath, and enjoy the literal antithesis of ski boots. The comfort and joy you feel lacing up a pair of snowboard boots is unmatched, in my opinion. Think of the biggest sneaker you ever wore, double the size by three, and you have this boot. Not only is walking around in snowboard boots far more comfortable but riding down the mountain in them is so much less stressful on your legs and feet. Now, don't let this dissuade you from trying skiing because it is still very fun, but for everyone I know who has tried both, the praise for these boots in contrast to ski boots is almost always positive. The same stiffness/skill/price spectrum applies here as with all the aforementioned equipment. The more expensive the boot, the more of an expert rider you need to be, and the more money you need to dish out. The biggest difference between ski boots and snowboard boots is that while there is only one type of ski boot, there are three kinds of snowboard boots: traditional lacing, speed lacing, and BOA lacing. Traditional lacing involves your massive shoelaces being woven along the toe and up the leg, certainly a good place for a beginner to start. While it may take more time to suit up, it is a reliable lacing system because it is very easily replaceable if one of the strings becomes frayed or damaged. The only downside in my experience is that they might not get as tight as you'd like them to be. The second method is speed lacing, which essentially has the strings prematurely laid throughout the boot. You pull the strings at the top, and it automatically tightens. In some models I've seen, there will be secular systems for the toe on top of the foot and then separately for the heel and the lower part of your leg. This will allow for specific tightening in these different areas should you so desire. Finally, we have the BOA system. This is the system I currently use. I find it the easiest and most effective in getting the tightest fit possible. Hovering right above the shin, it's a click and release circular knob. You twist it, and when you do, it pulls a series of metal wires around the boot tighter and tighter until you've reached your preferred stability. I love this method, and my goodness, it has served me well, but the one problem lies in replacing the wires should they break. It's a costly and frustrating thing to have happen because unless you take it to a shop, there's no way for you to fix it on the mountain should the necessity arise. In conclusion, the good thing about snowboard boots is that you have a nice selection to choose from. As the different kinds of boots have progressed through this tip, the price points also apply. More often than not, traditional lace will be the cheapest and moving up to BOA, which will be the most expensive. Like everything else on this list, find what you like, try it out, and eventually find what works best.

Tip 41: Speed vs. Comfort

Although I've talked about it a fair amount throughout this list, this bit of advice merits its own section. When talking about boots and bindings (and how they correlate with your skis or board), when you put aside stiffness as it relates to skill level, there is also a *deeper* level of detail that this concerns. It lies within the relation to the rider and their speed. When a board or ski is stiff, the bindings are stiff, and the boots are stiff...my goodness, you will go fast. Why? Because the rigidity of the collective equipment will give you a much more stable, much more speed-oriented ride. When you have a collection of gear whose directive is to be sturdy and hard-riding, you are going to go much, much faster, regardless of weight or size. When you have all-around softer gear (gear that isn't as stiff or rigid), not only will your agility increase, but the likelihood to go faster will also decrease. More flexible gear is better for beginners and those who are just starting, but it isn't limited to them. People who enjoy playful riding or terrain parks will sometimes adhere to more flexible gear for their freestyling needs. Then, you have people like me who enjoy a stiff ride, hard-charging and rocketing down a mountainside. While it is a small detail, it is important to note when choosing your gear.

Tip 42: Combo Purchase

Many enthusiast websites will offer boots/bindings combination purchases for occasionally discounted prices. This can be nice because, more often than not, the pairings are a set of boots and bindings that perform well together. It's also a good way to get the two pieces at well below the price that you could find on their brand websites. As the price for these increases, so will the quality of the equipment. I recommend using Evo.com for such purchases. I've used it twice in my life, and their suggestions have served me well up to this point. While you can still purchase these things separately, it could do a beginner well to seek out these types of deals. Cyber Monday is always my time of year where, if at all, I'll look to buy new equipment. With all that said, newcomers should try as best they can to find cheaper stuff to start on. For me, I always viewed my increasing skill as a self-milestone to earn the right to buy nicer, more expensive gear. It's a nice way to reward yourself, but don't break the bank right out of the gate (short of a nice pair of boots).

Style Isn't Everything, Warmth Is

Dress for Success

Tip 43: It's Called Fashion, Look It Up

All right! So, we've made it this far. We've covered what you need to ride down a mountain, now let's talk about what you need to wear down the mountain. There are two types of mountain fashion styles, in my opinion. First, we have form, and then we have function. From what I've seen on my mountain days, the outerwear of youthful riders will be flashy and fun. It's not to say that it's not keeping them warm, but at the same time, you don't necessarily need a $300 parka to keep you safe from sub-zero temperatures (says the guy who owns one). Then, you have older riders who tend to dress "traditionally" while riding. What I mean by that is proper snow pants, thermosensitive layering, and a tough outer shell. Depending on the time of year, styles can vary. On an early spring day, I've found myself with a t-shirt, hoodie, and football jersey keeping me warm when temperatures are in the mid-'30s; whereas, on an early January morning when it's ten below zero, I've been quadruple layered with my most expensive jacket on keeping the heat in. While the gear you ride is more objective, the stuff you wear is fairly subjective. A lot of it comes down to personal preference. For a larger guy like myself, I heat up pretty quickly when I'm exerting myself, so there are plenty of times where I won't be wearing as much as someone whose body doesn't heat up as easily. Like everything else, it varies, but here are some nice tips and bits of advice I can give to help you dress for the part.

Tip 44: Layer, Layer, Layer!

The way I start every mountain day (aside from a steaming cup of coffee and a hot shower—or hot tub) is laying out all of my gear and clothing for the day ahead. I'll talk about what I do for an ice-cold day as well as a warmer day. First, I have my compression shorts. I like them better than standard boxers or briefs because, realistically, a day on the mountain is a day-long workout. Exercise gear makes for a great base layer to wick away the sweat as the day wears on. Next, I'll throw on my long socks. These should go up past your calves and hug the top of the muscle. That way, they'll go the length of the boot and make sure that your legs don't brush up against your boots too hard. I recommend socks with a thicker thermal lining to keep your toes warm with ski boots. Ski boots are lined, but they can get pretty cold with snow running past them constantly. Snowboard boots are a tad warmer, but it never hurts to have the extra layer. After my socks, I'll apply my long underwear, which are also commonly referred to as "long Johns" by many people I've known in my life; maybe it's a Northeast thing. Long Johns will typically have a top and a bottom, so think thin sweat pants and a thin long sleeve shirt. After that, I'll have a pullover sweater on top and thicker sweats or joggers on the bottom. Next, we have the snow pants, and depending on where I am (or how far the mountain is), I'll lace up my boots, or at the very least, slide them on loosely. After that, I'll grab my gloves, goggles, and helmet, my big jacket, my bag, and my gear, and head to the slopes. As for a warmer spring day, as I said before, a simple shirt, hoodie, and football jersey (which acts as a nice makeshift windbreaker) will be more than enough to keep me warm. A sunny day when the temperature is that warm will heat you up pretty quickly. For some, that may be nice, but I overheat pretty quickly, given that I like to rip it down the mountain. The bottom line is always to check the weather before you go out. Bring a bag in case you need to shed a layer, or bring extras in case the temperature drops. Always be ready to adapt to the elements.

Tip 45: Basking in the Budget

Mountain sports aren't cheap. Seldom will you find any part of this experience as something that will be going easy on your wallet. Thankfully we're through the worst of it. Somewhere down the way, when you're all set with the gear you'll be riding, you'll only have to worry about the clothes on your back. It's nice, though, because you can buy clothing to keep you warm without destroying your budget. There are, of course, plenty of jackets out there that can total past $1000, but at the end of the day, cheap layering is your best friend. I'd recommend places like Target for the underlayer stuff and places like REI when they have clearance sales. Local ski shops in mountain areas also have great deals. Often, they'll also have used resale clothing, which is a great deal for beginners who don't want to dish out lots of money fresh out of the gate. Even for older or more seasoned riders, the cheaper stuff will serve well no matter what. Granted, the sometimes weathered gear may not last as long, but it serves as nice interim gear. It can also be fun to purchase retro gear to fit the 80s or 90s look. Like my home resort, many mountains have throwback weekends where everyone will dress up for the mountain to make it a bit more fun. Themes like that can always bring out a fun vibe of a time gone by.

Tip 46: Jackets

Ski and snowboard jackets can be put into two categories: shells and insulated. Shells are typically for people who like to use thicker layers underneath. They act as a protective outer layer to shield from moisture and wind and give you a bit more freedom in what you can wear underneath. It also allows for the shedding of layers should the need arise. Insulated jackets are a bit more technologically advanced. The "insulation" comes from a zip-on/zip-off inner layer that can be removable. The "nice" jacket I have employs similar technology. On days where it gets a little warmer, it's nice to have the option to remove that if I do choose to wear that on a given day. The insulated layers in most jackets tend to be very thick, and that heat can build up fast, even for those smaller riders. It's also good to note that jackets like these will have thicker pockets that retain heat; they're good for phones, which can sometimes shut down in extreme temperatures. Plus, there's nothing worse than your music shutting down midway through a run because of your phone turning off. When it comes to jackets and wanting to dish out money for high quality, stick to the name brands, not just for the quality, but the longevity. More often than not, they also have some good bargains. Patagonia, North Face, and Columbia are all very good options if you're not trying to spend over a grand on a shell.

Tip 47: Snow Pants

There is some redundancy when it comes to jackets and pants because the same logic applies. You either go for a shell or insulated lining. With pants, however, the lining can get tricky. For myself, I don't particularly prefer it. It gets bunched up, can be uncomfortable, and takes away from flexibility. Not only can the lining bunch up in your pants, but it can also bunch up whatever undergarments you may be wearing. The waterproof or water-resistant nature of snow pants is very important, more so for snowboarders (since some spend a fair amount of their days either wiping out or sitting down on the mountain), and helps to keep whatever you are wearing underneath nice and dry. On a spring day, you'll even see people in simple sweatpants and sometimes jeans. To be frank, I've tried both, and jeans are surprisingly comfortable on a warmer day. For these, I suggest Obermeyer. They have been my go-to for as long as I can remember. They resist the cold and moisture very effectively and act as a great shell.

Tip 48: Gloves vs. Mittens

Here lies an ongoing debate amongst riders, one that has been raging for decades: mittens or gloves? The answer (like everything else on this list) comes down to personal preference. With gloves, you have dexterity, you have the use of your individual fingers, and for a lot of snowboarders, it makes it easier to click yourself into your bindings. The biggest drawback to gloves is warmth. You have each of your fingers in their own encasings, and for that reason, you may find your fingertips going number after being out for too long on a cold day. On the other hand, you have mittens. While you may not have the practical use of all of your fingers, you have the warmth x10. I have even found myself removing my mittens on a chairlift because they've gotten too sweaty. My best advice is that if you have a pair of both, mittens are better for colder weather, and gloves are far more suitable for those warm days. Look into Dakine or GORE-TEX for their ability to keep moisture out and warmth in. You're looking at around a $100 price tag, depending on how boujee you want to go with it.

Tip 49: Helmets

Arguably the most important piece of equipment in your arsenal, a helmet is something you should never go without because, in many instances, this is something that will and can save your life. Skiing and snowboarding are fun, but you're traveling over 40 mph with very little to protect you. If you fall the wrong way, there's a good chance you'll hit your head in some way. Having that hard protective shell on your head can protect you from concussions, brain damage, and possible death. Unfortunately, it has become increasingly popular in recent years to go without a helmet. For reasons unbeknownst to me, people seem to think that it isn't cool to wear one? Truly, I don't know. There are plenty of trends that can be fun to follow, but this is one I would seriously advise against.

Choose the safe option if it's between your head being a little extra warm and saving your life. If you are going to look for a quality brand, I'd recommend Smith. They're very reputable in the industry and are very high-tech helmets. Some even come with built-in speakers as well. These can run anywhere from $150-350, but given that they can be potentially lifesaving and long-lasting, I say spend the money.

Tip 50: Goggles

Finally, we have my *favorite* piece of equipment. It is also one of the most important in addition to the helmet. Your goggles are how you perceive the world before you. They are how you see the slope and every inch of snow that you're going to ride. They help you determine where and how you're going to make your turns. Their importance lies in their ability to deflect air, remain unfoggy, and enhance your vision of the snow. A sunny day on the mountain means bright light reflecting off of luminescent, bright, frozen water. At any point when you remove your goggles, you'll find yourself squinting very hard because of the reflection. Polarized lenses are always the best, like any nice pair of sunglasses. They protect your eyes from UV rays, which can be magnified by sunlight bouncing off the sun. This also allows you to see every little detail of the snow you're riding, where it's solid, where it's loose, and where it's icy. I also recommend buying goggles that have replaceable lenses and taking a second lens to the mountain with you that would be suitable for lower light situations. On a cloudy day, it can be very hard to read the snow with little light, especially when you're traveling at high speeds. It pays to be prepared and would really benefit you. Technology has improved as well since I bought my first polarized goggles. My pair of Oakley's (that I've had for about ten years now) have clamp-in lenses, but companies like Smith have innovated tremendously to the point where magnetic lenses are now very popular. They're much easier to handle and much more convenient on the move, especially if you ride with a backpack and have them tucked away somewhere. I'm a ride-or-die Oakley supporter, and it's a brand I would happily suggest to any type of rider. Their gear is high quality and one of the top brands in the industry. For goggles, I would also recommend Smith or Anon. All these brands will realistically cost you anywhere from $200-400.

Chapter Review:

- Do your research, try out different equipment, find your fit and what works best for you.
- Learn the mountain, find your happy place, and discover where you can excel and have the most fun.
- Buy. Boots. First. Their longevity will benefit you in ways you can't imagine, and when the time comes to purchase your skis or board, you'll know how to ride it all the better, and your body will know how to respond.
- Forget pride; you don't need *the* coolest gear on the market. Bargain deals and discount prices are your friends early on. Wait to earn the good stuff (except for goggles, definitely dish out money for quality eyewear).
- *Enjoy the ride*. This is. Going to be such an amazing experience if you let it. Have fun with it. Have fun learning. Find the joy in every little moment. Fall nine times and get up ten. Experience the magic of what mountain life can be.

Chapter 2: Easier to Learn, but Harder to Master

Earn Your Turns

If You Pizza, When You Need to French Fry, You're Gonna Have a Bad Time

Tip 51: Getting Started on Skiing

Congratulations! We've made it this far! So, let's go a little further. Thus far, we've discussed every possible aspect of preparing for your mountain days, and since we have, it's time to get into the gritty details of how to put all that preparation to use. In this chapter, we will explore my top tips for how to ski. Much like everything else in this guide, these will be lessons and methods that I was taught when first learning how to ski, and I hope they benefit you as well.

Tip 52: Sign Up for a Professional Lesson

This might feel like straying from the path, given that this is a guidebook. Still, one of the most beneficial things to anyone's experience (as well as the experience of others with you, you'll come to find) is signing up for a personal lesson with a mountain pro. It's very similar to a lesson with a golf pro; one on one, personal, and focused. If you are a parent trying to teach a younger one how to ski, a few days in Ski School is highly encouraged. One's situation could be a family trip to Colorado; or something like a timeshare where you are traveling somewhere with friends. The adults can play while the kids are away (and under the care, tutelage, and watchful eye of professionals). While it may be a nice bonding experience with one's children, teaching them from scratch can be a tad frustrating. My parents dropped me at ski school for five days while they explored the mountains in Aspen, and when it came time for me to ride with them, I was all the better because of it. Thankfully, the school also made their experience much easier because I didn't require too much attention or help (something I'm sure they were very grateful for). Elsewhere, at a more advanced age, say, a teenager or young adult, a personal lesson with a pro is where you should go, for several reasons. The first is that the intimate time spent with someone who is trained will give you very hands-on learning. It is *so* beneficial because not only do you have someone who knows what they're talking about, but they know how to articulate that knowledge into teachable moments, the same as any professor in a classroom. Although a classroom may have more similarities to something like ski school, perhaps the appropriate word would be a tutor. Learning amongst others can have its advantages, but nothing beats one-on-one.

Tip 53: Try Not to Be the One to Teach Your Friends

Little story time here…as I've said before, over the years, I've had the wonderful privilege of taking numerous ski trips to beautiful destinations with many different friends of mine. During a handful of them, I've gotten to have loads of my own fun, but it's been fairly common that each time there has been at least one friend of mine who hasn't been as gifted on the mountain. I mentioned earlier the time when I taught myself how to snowboard. It was when my friend was learning how to ski, and although I tried to teach him, it was tough for me to adequately communicate my knowledge to him simply because I wasn't mature enough yet. Oddly enough, I ended up falling for a week straight teaching myself how to snowboard, but it paid off because it opened my eyes to a new passion. Nonetheless, other instances involved me having too big a heart to say no. When I was in Breckenridge, my friend had wanted to learn how to snowboard, and while I was excited to be at a big, new mountain, initially, I was more concerned with that than teaching him. It wasn't entirely fair to him because I had promised that I'd help him, so thankfully, I did before I got too carried away. I finally figured out how to communicate the fundamentals so that he would understand and even coined my own phrase (The Box Out Method), which I'll discuss more in the next chapter. The most frustration (and the most laughs) came in Snowmass with my other friend, who had neither skied nor snowboarded. At first, he tried to ski, and let's just say it was a complete disaster; I love him to death, but he couldn't hold his balance to save his life. Pro tip: don't ever lean backward on skis (something we'll touch on later). After that travesty, I spent three hours on the same slope trying to get his snowboarding to reach the minimum level of "acceptable," and after much blood, sweat, and tears (of laughter), he simply told me to go on. It was a humbling thing for him because he truly gave it his all, but in the end, there wasn't much I could do, even with my ability to teach having improved significantly. The moral of the story is this: if you go on an expensive ski trip far away, convince your inexperienced friends to spend the money on a one or two-hour lesson so that they have the basics to ride with their friends. You may think you're being kind, promising them that you'll help teach them, but it'll only end in frustration.

Tip 54: Learn the Relationship Between Medial and Lateral Edges

What is a medial edge? What is a lateral edge? In layman's terms, they are your skis' inner and outer edges. If memory serves, it's predominantly an anatomical term that refers to the rotation of the ankle, but to skiers, it refers to the carving, turning, and use of one's edges throughout a turn sequence. Your lateral edges are your outside edges, and your medial edges (by process of elimination) are your inside edges. At any given time during a turn, you will have one medial and one lateral edge engaged. These will alternate as you progress through your turns. If you're turning right, your left foot will be downhill, with your medial edge engaged, and your uphill right foot will have its lateral edge engaged. In contrast, a left turn puts your right foot downhill with its medial engaged and your uphill left foot lateral edge engaged. Understanding the kind of pressure you're supposed to feel, as well as where (on your feet) and when (during your turn) you're supposed to feel it, is the first step in understanding the mechanics of a turn when skiing. Much like I explained earlier, the type of skis that you end up purchasing will have a direct correlation to how much you can carve into these edges when you're turning. The harder and stiffer a ski (usually cambered) is, will affect your medials and laterals in your turns; or at least, it'll allow you to "feel" it more as you're pushing through your turn. Rockers have plenty of ability to carve; it just won't be as stable or precise as the cambered. Next up, we have one of the most fundamentally important tips in skiing, one that was instilled in me very early on, and happily enough, it involves two of my favorite foods!

Tip 55: Pizza and French Fry

The most common phrase amongst beginner skiers, there's a very simple reason why these two techniques are named after popular foods: easy for kids to remember! I thought it was so fun, but it taught me valuable lessons when I started. "Pizza" refers to your skis when you point your toes or tips inward, creating an almost triangle shape, hence the name. This occurs when you begin a turn and engage your downhill medial edge. The converging of your tips causes you to slow down. You'll see toddlers on a mountain practicing this a lot because it offers a sort of comfort and makes it so you don't go too fast. It's also quite common to see these younglings "snowplowing" down the mountain, essentially pizza-ing straight down the mountain without turning at all, simply because they haven't mastered it yet. When you "french fry," your skis become parallel. This occurs after the turn and is where you'll find the most comfort on the mountain. During your large "S" turns, the moment when you french fry is when you're coasting across a trail, only to inevitably turn again. When you're in this parallel state, you'll find that you're not holding any particular edge, simply riding on the flats of your skis before you lean into your edge on the other side of the trail. The more experience you get, the more you'll find yourself french frying instead of pizza-ing. You'll notice your turns become more petite and precise, much like a rocking chair going back and forth instead of large, semi-truck-like, wide turns. Not only that, you'll find yourself more comfortable with speed. The speed will pick up immensely when your skis are parallel and pointed downhill. Some people are even so expert and comfortable that they don't take turns down a slope, even on the steepest of runs. Once you have mastered these two elements, it opens up your learning to fine-tuning your skills.

Tip 56: Weight Dispersal (Lean Forward!!!)

The human body has a natural disposition to want to be upright. It helps us keep balance, feel comfortable, and safe. However, skiing is one of the last things you should do with skiing. When people like my friend in Snowmass first start skiing, those whose balance isn't fully realized yet will have a hard time staying upright and will naturally feel the need to lean backward going down a slope since that will feel most comfortable. In skiing, the key is to lean forward. The straps on the shin portion of your boots are there for a reason, as you're meant to lean into them, hard. Not only does this keep you stable when you're riding, but it also gives you more control over the control of your edges. It eases your ability to lean into turns and carve because God forbid, you try to lean back; essentially, you'll "Charlie Brown" and feel your feet come out from under you as you land hard on your backside. It's not a pleasant feeling, but it can happen with beginners. Your forward leaning is also going to incorporate your arms. I mentioned ski poles earlier and that they're not necessary and even not recommended for beginners because understanding one's body and balance is a key part of starting. If you ski without poles, you'll find your arms at a nice ninety-degree angle, somewhat separated from your sides, as a natural response to feeling unbalanced. When you incorporate poles, it tends to offer a bit more comfort, in my experience. Not only that, but you'll feel more inclined to lean forward since the positioning of the poles offers side-to-side balance vs. the forwards/backward balance that you should already be experiencing.

Tip 57: Bend. Your. Knees.

One of *the* most important aspects of skiing and snowboarding is what you do with your knees. Think of them as shocks on the underside of a car. The stiffer the shocks are, the rougher and bumpier the ride will be, and the more stable the ride will be in tight turns and corners. The more loose the shocks are, the smoother the ride will be, but you'll experience more body roll in the corners, not as much stability. The same applies to a rider's legs, and more specifically, their knees. Your legs act as the shocks in this scenario. When a car comes to a screeching halt, the breaks lock up, and the shocks stiffen and almost harden. If you treat your skis as your breaks and your legs as your shocks, the same will occur on the mountain. You may swerve out of control and lose the ability to stop yourself safely. *Never* lock out your knees because it will spell nothing but trouble for you if you do. There is a good chance you'll open the door for a possible injury to occur, and when it comes to your knees, I don't think I need to explain why that would be bad or why they are crucial to mountain sports. Keep your knees bent at all times. Let them flex with the mountain. It lets you feel the run you're riding down a little more efficiently. It also allows for better control of your skis. Be the one to control them; don't stand upright, stiff as a board, and let them take you for a ride. If you do, chances are, you'll hurt yourself. Feel the flexing of your knees at every turn. Let them give to the bumps and moguls in the snow. If you go off even a small rise with your legs too straight, you might find yourself gaining an unwanted lift off of the slope; if you're not comfortable with being in the air, this could certainly present an issue. Skiing takes more of a toll on your legs than snowboarding does. While boarding may work the undersides of your feet and the lower part of your calves, your thighs remain relatively at ease, in my experience. For that, I advise heavy offseason training if you wish to keep up with continuous mountain days, which brings us to our next segment.

Tip 58: Train Your Body and Mind

Luckily, I'm not here to teach you how to have a tight workout regimen; we're here to learn how to ski and snowboard. That being said, I do have some advice about keeping your body ready for the mountain. After the Super Bowl, whether you're the winning or losing team, do you think it's safe to say that either side takes the next couple of months off? After their multi-million-dollar contract extension, do they just lounge on a beach with cocktails? Heck NO! These men are in the weight room and on the practice field the very next week, if not the next day! I implore a similar mindset to anyone committed to advancing their skills on the mountain. Year-round training will benefit your abilities in ways that, frankly, I wish I had applied earlier in my life. There was a time midway through high school when I found myself exhausted and sore on an otherwise average trip to my house in Maine. Sometime after that, I started stretching more and doing more lower body positive work that I knew would eventually help me when skiing. I practiced several yoga poses in the mornings for stretching, no less than four days a week. This opened up the muscles in my hips and, more importantly, my legs, specifically, my quads and my hamstrings. I also practiced stretching the arches of my feet. Finally, I would do knee mobility exercises to keep them limber and active, in addition to my normal gym routine. It's important to keep your body in check, especially for a sport as demanding as skiing. You need some sturdy and strong thighs to handle long days on the mountain, and that demand will only increase as your skills increase. The steeper the slope, the more your body will ask of you.

Tip 59: Don't Bite Off More Than You Can Chew

As you're well aware by now, every piece of information I've shared thus far has been important, not only for the education of mountain sports beginners but to keep you safe as well. Here, I want to talk briefly about your mindset when you first start. I have ridden with beginners of all shapes, sizes, and, most importantly: confidence levels. I've known some who can't stomach vertical incline and will stick to the bunny slopes for days on end before they even feel remotely comfortable enough to venture elsewhere. Then, in some cases, I've been with beginner friends who cannot wait to ride higher, faster, and harder as soon as possible, regardless of whether or not they fall flat on their faces. Some have a fear of heights; others need speed. My advice to *you* is: Take. Your. Time. The mountain will be there, as my mother would tell me. Take time to learn and to grow. You don't need to be jumping to any conclusions or ego-driven rides down the mountain on too steep an incline. I learned this the hard way when I first started snowboarding. I took a trip to Sunday River in Maine with my good friend (the one I learned how to snowboard with while he skied). Sunday River is one of the largest resorts in Maine, with up to seven peaks and hundreds of trails to offer. At one point later in the day, we were feeling quite confident in our abilities and decided to take on a trail that was very aptly named "Agony." That is no joke, that is a real trail, and we thought it would be a brilliant idea to go down it, guns blazing, with hearts full of courage. We were very hastily humbled.

Agony is a double black diamond and an entirely straight shot down the mountain. We went in hot and came out cold. What I mean is that I caught a toe edge no more than fifty feet down the slope and faceplanted hard. This wasn't the end of it though. I then proceeded to slide on my stomach down this icy groomer for about 200+ feet. My friend had joined me in a similar predicament as we looked up at people in the chairlift seats cheering us on. In all seriousness, I was sliding for so long that my headphones took me through an entire song for the duration of the aforementioned sliding. While it was fun, it was also extremely humble!

Tip 60: Have Patience, and Have Fun!

With any new sport, hobby, or practice, mastering a form of art will take time. It took me years, even having started as a child, to fully master my abilities and understand my body when it came to skiing. I fell a lot, I hit a fair number of trees, and I even faceplanted on hard icepack more times than I care to mention, but I still held a strong feeling inside me: persistence. I kept going because I wanted to be better. Finally, in time I did, I saw the fruits of my labor come full circle. It became so rewarding to witness my hard work pay off as the years went on. It's what allowed me to take on the big mountains in the West and continue to learn in the East. It's as they say, "Learn to ski on ice, and you can ski anywhere." The best part of it all is that I'm still learning. Much like golf professionals through the years, there is always learning to be done. So with that in mind, keep at it, even when things seem tough, even when you fall hard and have to call it a day. Keep getting back up, and you will see that your experience will become that much more fulfilling through your hard work. Have patience, and push yourself only when appropriate; you'll be amazed at what you can accomplish on the slopes.

Tip 61: Racers vs. Twin Tips

I briefly touched upon this in earlier sections regarding different brands of skis, but I wanted to take a moment to go more into depth about it. There are racer skis, and there are twin tips. The section mentioned above about stiffer skis and more flexible skis can be correlated here. More often than not, you'll find racer skis being extremely stiff and sturdy. They're for the traditionalists, the speed demons, those who pay diligence to the sport. At least, that is the stereotype that surrounds them. In reality, anyone can ride on racers; however, it is not the type of ski I'd hand over to a beginner. Therein lies the twin tips. These are fun ones. The "play around" skis. The skis for the park junkies, the freestylers, and more youthful types. Where racers have their directional tips, tips with flat tails, a raised nose, and hard-cutting edges, the twins offer lifts in both nose and tail. Their edges, while able to carve, offer more playful feedback. They are the more forgiving of the two variants, and what I'd suggest for first-timers. While twin tips can be rough and rigid, like my Faction 2.0's, they commonly are not as tough as their aggressive, distant cousin. Beginners need a soft experience so as not to sway them from progress. Upon reaching a level of skill that has increased the rider's comfort, it is not uncommon to transition to racers, but they only adhere to a particular style of skiing. Even when someone has become more advanced in their riding, they may simply seek more advanced twin tips. Such was the case with myself. I learned on basic twin tips, eventually tried to get used to racer skis, and eventually found myself back in twin tips. It comes down to the acquired taste of the rider's style, something that all of you will learn about in time.

Tip 62: Powder vs. Pack

Remember when I talked about always leaning forward? The importance of leaning forward narrows down to your control. You keep your heel planted in the back of your boot. You feel the pressure in the front of your legs, in your lower quads, just above the knees, just above your shocks. The forward-leaning pressure allows you to easily and effortlessly direct your tips when you are in motion. Although the pressure is being pushed forward, the reason why that pressure lets you direct your skis is that the force is being planted through the back of your feet, through your heels. While this is an appropriate lesson in how to ride hard-packed, groomed snow, the playbook switches up a little bit when you're talking about powder skiing. In powder, you're riding on a light and fluffy surface, and because of that, you need to treat it very differently. Since you'll be "floating" on this powder, leaning too far forward, especially in deeper powder, is going to lead to your nose tips dipping too deep. When this happens (and I'm speaking from experience here), you are most certainly going to front flip into the deep snow and even possibly disconnect yourself from your ski bindings. There's less control in powder skiing, but you must allow yourself to be carried. "Go where the wind blows you," as they say. You'll find more control in leaning back slightly, just as you would if you were water skiing. When you lean back, you give even more power to your heels, and they act as something of a rudder when surfing over that beautiful, seamless, fresh powder. It's also a bit more relaxing riding on this vs. hardpack, but try not to think about having less control on it because the biggest plus side is that if you fall, it's like falling into the world's biggest (and coldest) pillow.

Tip 63: More of a Suggestion Than a Rule

Yet again, here is something that, while I've previously mentioned, deserves a section of its own. Let us recall how I discussed ski length as it relates to rider height. While it is important to begin your journey with skis adequate for your height, there is nothing wrong with trying something off the beaten path. I've said it many times, but the further you go into this journey, the more you'll learn about yourself. You'll come to understand your body better and how it reacts to equipment. There's no shame or breaking of the rules if you find yourself a more adequate rider on shorter skis. You also may find that you'll have more maneuverability or an easier time turning. It's trial and error, but in time, simply find what you feel most comfortable on!

Tip 64: From the Fat "S" to the Thin "S" (image?)

When you're learning the basics of turning, you will be taking massive turns on the widest runs that a resort has to offer. Nice and winding, long and wide, as well as slow. The pizza/french fry method will serve you well for a good while until you start to shorten your turns and tighten them. In time you'll get more comfortable with speed. I spoke earlier about how your turn style will evolve the faster you go. With more speed comes more precise turns. You won't be taking wide angles or aggressively leaning into your medials and laterals. Instead, you'll be lightly leaning back and forth between them. Seeing an experienced skier at full speed is a truly beautiful thing to watch. It's pure, untethered, uninterrupted riding. You can see how they rock back and forth, transferring pressure from foot to foot, side to side. Gone will be the days angling your tips inward as you progress through a turn. Keep this in mind as you find more confidence. Soon you'll be carving so effortlessly, you'll hardly feel the pressure and rising soreness in your thighs. The nature of your turns is your first step to self-recognition and realizing how far you've come.

Tip 65: Chairlift Etiquette

One of the trickiest and yet most important areas (for safety purposes) on a mountain is getting on and off the chairlift. Most traditional ski resorts will have anywhere from a couple to over a dozen chairlifts that ferry riders to the different peaks for them to ride down. Very old-school, traditional riders may want to earn their turns and hike to the tops of peaks to then ski down, time-consuming labor that satisfies the purest of skiers. As I've said before, I've only done it once. I wouldn't do it consistently, but it does offer a feeling of satisfaction; enough of that, though. Ninety-nine percent of your time will be spent riding chairlifts up the mountain, and there are some things you should know. As you enter the line for the chairlift, the workers at the lifts will direct you into groups. Chairlifts carry anywhere from two to four people, with very few holding five or six. The larger capacity lifts are otherwise known as gondolas, where you store your gear on the outside of the lift and sit inside, warm from the elements. You'll only find these on the bigger mountains, so more often, you'll find yourself riding an open-air chair. As you're directed through these lines, you'll be put as a single rider, a duo, trio, or quadruple. When you're at the front of the line, make sure you've unhooked the straps of your poles from your wrists and are carrying them in both hands. Keeping them attached while you're on the chair can be dangerous and potentially yank you off the chair, which could lead to serious injury. You'll be guided to the line where the next chair will rotate around and be guided to you by the operators. Make sure to stand upright, still, and with patience. When the chair reaches you, sit down gently as the chair lifts you and your friends off your feet. Hold your poles in between your legs, or like some, fashion them underneath yourself in between your legs, and parallel to them. Lower the guard rail for safety once you are some space out from the lift station. Sometimes the lift may come to a sudden halt if someone at a loading station falls; it stops you from being jolted forward unexpectedly. Some of them also have bars where you can rest your feet instead of having your boots hang. As you ride the chairlift, enjoy the view! Get your playlist ready if you choose to listen to music as you ride, hydrate, even cool off your potentially sweaty hands (I find myself doing this often). Refrain from knocking loose snow off your boots and skis onto skiers below. If you have snacks or drinks with you, don't litter either. Too often do

I see trash on the mountain, and it's always disappointing. The final tower supporting the cables on the chairlift will often have a sign telling you that it's time to lift the bar. As you do, brace yourself to make contact by keeping your ski tips up and your body narrow. You don't want to accidentally bump into anyone getting off with you since it can cause a bit of a jam and a possible wipeout. Next thing you know, you're off! Ready to ride down the slopes.

Tip 66: My First Time (Part I)

I have only spoken in passing about the first time I experienced what it was like to go skiing, but I feel that it is good to share the full story. Nearly twenty years ago, at the mere age of seven, while living in Texas, my parents thought it would be a fun idea to go on a trip. At first, they toyed with the notion of going back to the Northeast, to our roots, to visit family and explore. They also thought of making a Grand Canyon road trip—which we ended up doing a few years later. Eventually, they concluded that a ski trip would be an excellent idea. They had spent most of their lives skiing in various parts of the world and finally decided it was time for me to learn. They had coordinated the trip with two families of old friends whose kids I had befriended at a very young age when we lived in Oklahoma. Since we have always traditionally been a road trip, they pondered the idea but quickly realized that a flight would be much easier. We packed up our bags and set out to our destination: Aspen, Colorado. I remember looking out the window of the airplane and seeing the vastness of the Rocky Mountains for the first time. As a kid, I was awestruck at the landscape I saw before me. I thought stuff like this only existed in The Lord of the Rings. Thankfully, I learned that those were filmed in New Zealand, which inspired a future travel experience for me. As we arrived at our hotel, my two friends and I set up in our room. As little kids will do, we had our own fun area to stay and play in while the parents had their separate rooms.

Tip 67: My First Time (Part II)

The suite they had reserved was massive and had a full kitchen and everything! It was the first fancy hotel I ever remember staying at as a kid. We had arrived sometime during the mid-afternoon, and it made for a nice viewing experience of the space around us. They planned accordingly and got us a "ski-in/ski-out" living space. This means that at any moment, we could walk off the edge of our patio right onto a ski slope that would take us directly to the nearest ski lift. We threw on our bathing suits and skittishly made our way to the hot tub. We'd never seen so much snow, nor had we ever been in such a cold place before with so little clothing. We found ourselves laughing so hard our bellies hurt, which only seemed to make us colder before we eventually submerged ourselves in the hot water. It was so blissful and so peaceful, feeling so relaxed in such a setting. The kids are so easily entertained, with the parents enjoying their glasses of wine looking on. Our parents were informing us of the days ahead, how we were going to go on our own adventure, how, in the following days, we would be attending ski school. However, we were confused and weren't sure what to think of it. In our naïve, childlike nature, we assumed we'd have homework! How absurd, right? The not surprising talk coming from kids. They told us our teacher would be taking us on adventures around the mountain and that we'd be having normal days like school, but that instead of classes, we'd be outdoors in the mornings and afternoons! Plus, a lunch break in between. As the night wore on, we excitedly readied ourselves for bed and the day ahead.

Tip 68: My First Time (Part III)

The time had come! We woke up bright and early, as hyped-up kids do, much like Christmas morning. The feeling was almost identical. Our parents ferried us down to the rental shop to get our boots and skis fitted. It was my first time putting on ski boots, and I was shocked at just how rigid and tight they were. I did, however, find it amusing to walk around in them since they were so stiff. The awkward heel/toe walk I had to execute made me giggle, but before long, my folks had brought me to what did feel like a lower school classroom, with lots of colorful ski posters from the 1980s. I remember being so excited to get started. Our instructor gave us a fairly lengthy introduction before he walked us out to a nice, flat area. This was where we began practicing our turns and understanding the feeling of our edges. Frankly, I don't remember falling, but it's safe to say that I did. I remember them telling us about the pizza and french fry metaphors, frequently shouting them up the hill at us. I don't remember it being the most hands-on training, but it was enough to get us all going. Soon after, we set out for our first bunny slope. Not to toot my own horn or anything, but I came to find I was pretty good at this, even receiving praise from my instructors. The rest of the day was spent on the green trails, and to my parent's joy, they came to find that I had excelled on my first day. They were just as excited as I was for the following four days of school and to see just how far my newfound talent could go.

Tip 69: My First Time (Part IV)

During the next several days, our journeys took us to the furthest reaches of the mountains. We explored Ajax and Buttermilk and took on many high-altitude green circle trails, but before the end of the week, the instructors recognized that we were ready for the next step. The temperature that final day was well below freezing, and a massive storm front had moved in. The snow falling from the sky was thick; the snowflakes were large and heavy. It was my first true blizzard experience, but it made for outstanding conditions. Although I'd spent a few Christmases in the Northeast, I'd never seen something quite like this. They took us a bit higher up on Buttermilk to some of the blue squares, where tree cover was scarce. It opened up the trails to more snowfall. They took us on a winding trail with glades better suited to beginners at one point. I remember being so excited and being just a little too confident in my recently discovered talents. I got some speed going, somewhat ahead of the group, and found my way to a medium-sized jump. I thought I had a handle on the situation; I thought I was in control, but little did I know, my visibility wasn't all there. Due to the thick snowfall, there was something I didn't see until it was too late. Midway through the jump, as I was flying through the air, there was a low-hanging branch. I think you can guess what happened next! I flew straight into the branch! It hit me square in the chest and completely table-topped me. Thank *God* for the heavy snow, because were that ice instead, I would have been seriously injured. My epic wipeout was met with plenty of laughs and smiles and has been kept for a great story ever since.

Tip 70: My First Time (Part V)

If I'm being perfectly honest, I don't think I realized just how big of an impact this trip would have on me until years later. I found something meaningful to me, something that would forever change me. It inspired something deep inside me that very few things in my life have since: a passion that would drive my commitment to get better. This inspiration would fuel the desire that has filled twenty years of wanderlust to seek out the most beautiful and awe-inspiring mountaintops and conquer them. There are very few sports or hobbies where you find yourself in control of what happens as much as skiing or snowboarding can. It may seem like you vs. the mountain, but it is you vs. yourself in reality. It's a statement of how far you are willing to push yourself, to seek the most of what you can physically and mentally achieve. My hope for anyone who undergoes such a process is to find a love for it in themselves as I have for myself, and I wish anyone luck who chooses that path.

Chapter Review:

- Consult a professional. Even when you've broken the bank on a trip, go a little further. The benefits far exceed the cost.
- Go on a trip with experienced friends, but spend time alone. Learn how your body reacts when you're not worried about the onlooking of others, especially people you know.
- Master control over your edges. Master the Pizza and the French Fry. Lean forward and feel the pressure in your quads.
- Bend your knees at all costs. Let them be the measure of the force you apply to the slope through your skis. It's your most valuable asset.
- Make the offseason productive. Train your body so that you're just as excited as you are physically prepared when the time comes.

Chapter 3: Harder to Learn, but Easier to Master

It's All in the Hips

A Sore Posterior is the Sign of a Good Learning Day

Tip 71: Change of Direction (Literally)

Perhaps the most noticeable transition from skiing to snowboarding (which confused me at first) was that instead of facing directly down the mountain, you're facing ninety degrees in the other direction. Whether you ride with your left foot downhill (regular) or your right foot downhill (goofy), you have to adapt to a completely different physical orientation. One of the reasons why skiing is recognized as "easier to learn, harder to master" is because of the comfort that the forward-facing ride offers. Since snowboarding is of the "harder to learn, easier to master" variety, much of this learning curve comes in the form of turning your body just a tad one way or the other. For someone like myself, it was very difficult at first to understand how to perfect this. I'll talk more about it, but there were many times when I had considered giving up because of all the falls I was taking. The first week of teaching myself, I think there were two separate occasions where I was convinced I had broken my wrists. I'd fallen on my butt more times than I care to mention, and it hurt to sit down for about a week, but thank God for hot tubs. Sometime earlier in the guide, I briefly mentioned past athletic experience. While it may help your snowboarding education to have skateboarded or surfed at some point in your life, the big adjustment in transitioning from those to the mountain is becoming comfortable with having your feet locked into the type of board you're riding. My good friend (the surfer)—who became a great boarder under my tutelage—was able to find comfort fast because of the similarities between the sports; however, the greatest difficulty was realizing that his feet didn't have mobility on a snowboard vs. a surfboard. Despite this obstacle, he found it easy to overcome because he already understood what it felt like to ride sideways. This section is mainly for those who (like me) learned to ski first. The change of direction takes time to adjust to, but it won't be as big of a challenge for those starting with boarding.

Tip 72: Start Very, Very Small

As the chapter suggests, your beginnings in this sport vs. skiing will be significantly harder. Although skiing allows for some minor degree of steepness, I highly suggest beginning on the smallest incline you can find. With skiing, you will go faster. That is a guarantee no matter what. The thing that offers comfort with the speed of skiing is the fact that the body's natural reaction to wanting to slow down will lead you to pizza. It feels natural, and therefore the pointing of your toes will bring you to a halt. With snowboarding, your body requires far more focus and coordination to stop. Since this is the case, begin on the bunny slopes. Heck, begin on the "bunny" bunny slopes. The beginning of the bunny slopes is where you'll find two-year-olds starting. This is not only going to be crucial in your snowboarding experience, but it's going to prolong your patience for the tedious learning experience that lies before you. The low to minimal incline will help you understand your board and your body in a far more learning conducive environment than even the easiest of bunny slopes. It will also allow for very easy-going falls because you will inevitably fall in your first few days. Our next section will prepare you for the inevitable and make it a bit easier for you to avoid injury. Have some grit though; it's not always going to tickle!

Tip 73: Tie a Little String, Understanding the Heel/Toe Relationship (Part I)

Some of the most useful advice I received in the beginning was somewhat of a visual metaphor. My instructor told me: pretend as though there is an invisible string tied around your big toe and that it reaches to the back of your heels. This type of visual learning helped me understand that the heel-to-toe relationship in snowboarding is one of the most important aspects to understand. Unlike the medial and lateral edges of skiing, snowboarding involves forward and backward-facing edges, defined as heel and toe edges. When you're on the flat "bunny" bunny slopes, as I've previously mentioned, the first thing you'll learn how to do is how to control this relationship. You'll begin sitting down. Using your arms, and with the help of an instructor, you'll be brought to your feet. You'll be facing downhill, imagining your toe pulling at the back of your heel as it lifts off the ground. The exercise you should practice here will have your arms extended for balance, with your knees bent and the upward pulsing of your toes. This will give you an idea of the control you have over your board. Picture it as flaps on an airplane wing going up and down. The flatter the flaps (and feet), the faster you'll glide forward. The higher the flaps (and toes) are angled, the slower you go, with more drag. This will cause your heel edge to dig into the snow more, allowing you to control your speed. Practicing this motion will lead you to a more stable riding. Much of the time, you'll see newcomers practicing this. The more you pulse your toes, the more you'll understand its effect. It'll also strengthen the arches in your feet which will pay dividends down the line. Next to your calves, they're the strongest and most important muscles when snowboarding. As you're practicing your pulses, you may find one end of your board starting to point downhill. Fret not, this may lead to some of your first falls, but we're not worrying about turning just yet. Nor are we worrying about which foot we're putting downhill (just yet), but in time that will come. If we'll recall, that's what we refer to as riding "regular" and riding "goofy."

Tip 74: Tie a Little String, Understanding the Heel/Toe Relationship (Part II)

Now that we've come to understand what controlling your heel edge entails, let's discuss the other edge (and my personal favorite one to ride on), the toe edge! It remains partial to a rider's preference, some like the heel more, some like the toe more, but for me—one with a very strong lower body—it is where I excel in my riding. I also find this part of riding to be a bit easier. The way you can practice it on these flat slopes is essentially the reverse of heel riding, but instead of lifting your toes, you're pressing them down into the snow while the back of your heel lifts off the ground. Think of the anchor of the string being attached to your heel as it actively pulls your toe into the snowpack. For someone like me, I can apply more pressure through my toes than my heels. It lets me carve low and very deep in my turns. It lets me push hard and aggressively through them. First-time riders might also find that it's easier to find balance on the toe edge when facing uphill. It allows a little more flexing in the knees and naturally more strength driven through the front of your legs instead of the rear. For folks like me, pushing through a toe edge is the easiest way to initiate a turn. I ride my heels for a short time to one side of the mountain and aggressively push through my toe edge to send me soaring across the other side of the trail. As you progress through your skills, you'll find which are better for you. Everyone has their strengths and their preferences, and so much like the rest of this journey, you'll come to find what yours are as well.

Tip 75: Learn How to Fall (Part I)

Have you ever played a contact sport? Hockey? Lacrosse? Rugby? In high school, for me, it was football. I found a love for the sport early in my life watching Tom Brady lead the New England Patriots to numerous championships (thank God my father is from Boston—I recognize that I grew up a lucky sports fan). When middle and high school came around, I decided to give it a go. As it turned out, I loved it, and better yet, I was good at it! This was the first time I'd tried a sport aside from a mountain sport that I found a talent for. I was big, quick on my feet, and found it fun to tackle people, but therein lay an art form within the sport: form tackling. We would spend countless hours each week learning how to properly tackle on the field. It was an arduous process but beneficial when game time came because it assured us when we were running into each other and tackling, we would remain safe and not seriously injured. Sure, we'll end up with some bruises, but that's half the fun! The same applies to snowboarding. While you may fall when you ski, the frequency that occurs is next to none. With boarding, especially in the beginning, you're going to be continuously learning that even when you get going, you're going to fall. It won't always be pleasant, but it's manageable. This will be one of the most useful tips for when you start to board because it will keep you physically in the game and mentally assist you. Without it, there's a good chance you'll want to give up much sooner than you should.

Tip 76: Learn How to Fall (Part II)

In the simplest of terms, there are two ways to fall: forwards and backward. Unless your nose dips into *very* deep powder, it's unlikely that you're going to do a sideways front flip. If you catch a toe edge, falling forward has its dangers. If done improperly, you're likely to break one or both of your wrists, and if you haven't braced your arms, you also may hit your face on the snowpack. Your helmet protects your head, but aside from your goggles and the occasional balaclava (facemask), your face isn't going to have much to soften the fall. If you find yourself "catching a toe," do your best to let your knees bend. In my first couple of years, I wore kneepads for this very reason. When you catch a toe edge, the full force and weight of your body are thrown forward against your will. People tend to tense up when they're learning. Your knees may lock up, which opens the door for an even harder faceplant. If you loosen your knees, your body rolls downward instead of slamming down. It not only loosens the overall impact but makes it easier for the next part. The next step is knowing what to do with your hands and arms. Do NOT straighten your arms to try to catch yourself. Forget the broken wrists; you're looking at shattered and dislocated elbows. Think of this process like a bottom-to-top rolling of the body. Catch the toe, start at the bending of the knees, followed by the bending of the arms, and let your hands hit the ground first, almost sliding them down the mountain as your elbows eventually make contact. In my experience, this has been the softest and most forgiving way to fall forward. What comes next is much harder and, frankly, the more dangerous way to fall. Best to be prepared.

Tip 77: Learn How to Fall (Part III)

You had to know this was coming; if you can fall forwards, you can certainly fall backward too! While the process of falling forward has an easy method (in my opinion) to help sway you from serious injury, falling backward can be a bit trickier. It also can be far more dangerous. A fall backward can lead to a bad tailbone injury (speaking from firsthand experience), a back injury, or worst of all: a head injury. If you ever find yourself catching a heel edge, the first thing you should always remember is to tilt your head forward and brace for the impact. Even though the force of hitting the ground will likely push your head towards the ground, angling it forward will reduce the likelihood of whiplash and concussion. The "bracing" of yourself comes with the tightening of your core and the conscious awareness of protecting your head. Your helmet will absorb a majority of the blow, but it will hurt nonetheless. Bending your knees can help in this situation, but it isn't as important as it is when falling forward. At the very least, it will shorten the distance between your head and the ground. When bending your knees, I like to angle my elbows backward. Don't fully extend your arms; otherwise, you risk a shoulder dislocation (also speaking from experience). With the bracing of your body, the leaning of your head, the bending of your elbows, and the realization that this is going to hurt, there's a good chance that you'll walk away with nothing more than bruises. As I learned in the beginning, it does take time to learn how to withstand this impact safely. All it is is part of the process. It introduces some grit to the scenario and—for me at least—makes it a bit more fun. I've had my fair share of wipeouts, but thankfully none to this point that put me out of commission. Remember: fall nine times, get up ten!

Tip 78: Regular or Goofy?

Snowboard riders are defined by their riding style. Skiers don't have a say in the matter aside from the occasional backward riding, but for boarders, they must discover what their dominant foot is. Riding regular indicates that your left foot is downhill and can often be seen in right-hand dominant riders. The opposite applies for goofy riders, where the right foot will be downhill instead, usually alluding to the fact that they are left-hand dominant. In this particular aspect of snowboarding, that past athletic experience that I spoke of earlier comes into play. That being said, my good friend (the surfer) rides his surfboard goofy but rides regular on a snowboard. It simply comes down to personal preference and what feels most comfortable; everyone is different. The distinction between right and left hand—or in this case, foot—dominant usually adheres to the rider's physically stronger leg. Since I ride regular, I know my right leg is stronger, while my left leg is what directs me, allowing my uphill leg to be the force that drives me through my turns. Play around with it, see what feels better for you. It's all part of the learning experience. Our next section will discuss something that can be a "learn as you go" sort of talent. Even after a decade of riding regular, I still find it difficult to ride.

Tip 79: Riding Switch (Ambidextrous Riding)

Switch! The ability to ride switch is the mark of a heavily seasoned, experienced, and talented snowboarder. Simply put, it is when a rider can switch between regular and goofy riding. For them, it doesn't matter how you start or finish a run, but everywhere in between, it is likely that they'll utilize both styles. Riding switch also means that a rider will probably be using a specific type of board, which is more often than not a true twin board, meaning that it is the same design in the front and rear of the board, allowing for seamless transitions between the two. Avid switch riders also tend to gravitate towards the terrain parks, in my experience. Much of the time, those I see in the parks will be bouncing back and forth between them. It lets them land their jumps much more comfortably since you may enter a jump one way and land it in a completely different fashion. While I advise trying your hand in either style, focus with your dominant side first; i.e., if you write, kick, throw right-handed, start practicing regular first. Only when you've mastered one style or the other should you try riding switch. It's not a necessary thing to learn but can make your mountain days pretty fun and creative.

Tip 80: Overlap—Some Things That Apply for Skiing Apply Here

It's not all specific to skiing or snowboarding! There are a lot of things that overlap between the two sports. The first of which that I'd like to implore is *taking a professional lesson*. In my mind, this may be more important for snowboarding than it is for skiing. That only comes with the "harder to learn" aspect of it. It's awkward, it's uncomfortable, and for those who have never been on any type of board, it's a wholly bizarre experience. I am, of course, speaking from my own time initially learning how to board. Take the time to listen to someone who really knows how to show you the ropes. It will be frustrating and probably will test your patience, but it's worth it! Recall my tip about leaning forward when skiing; it's a bit different with snowboarding. There's an interesting element to how and where you should lean when riding. Generically, you would want to feel about as centered as possible. Lean too far forward, and you're going to lose control of your nose tip and wipeout. Lean too far backward, and you're going to "Charlie Brown" and feel the board come out from underneath you, neither of which are pleasant. Find the middle ground and center your weight on the board. That being said, don't be afraid to lean back a little. I mentioned it earlier, but I like to charge. That's my style of snowboarding. Deep carves with big, wide turns. I like going fast and getting low. In specific contexts like this, it's okay to lean back—but only a little. What I said earlier still applies. When your skills are evolving, you'll come to understand what your "middle ground" feels like. Just make sure to take it slow and that your balance comes to you naturally.

When finding your balance—as with skiing—*bend. your. knees.* Do you think it was important for skiing? Multiply that importance by about ten. If you stiffen like a board *on your board*, you are asking for real trouble. Not only does the bending of your downhill knee indicate how hard you're able to charge, but the bending of your uphill knee dictates all the control you have in your turns and how you carve. So while it matters in skiing, the knee bending in snowboarding directs far more than just acting as your shocks or suspension on the mountain. Board size will also not always correlate to your height or weight. As I've said, my first board was extremely short and perhaps one of the fatter boards available to purchase today. However, my talents evolved, and so did my preference for a longer, stiffer board. While I enjoy the Jones I ride now; the YES is still my favorite and most unique board I have ever ridden. I suggest heavy research to seek out what kinds of boards you will enjoy, but there is no strict guideline for what kind of board you should buy, simply what you will feel most comfortable on. The big "S" and little "S" or the fat and the thin ones you'll create when riding down a trail will be similar to those of skiing. Instead of your big, wide turns, you will find them narrowing to a winding sort of pattern. I find it a bit more enjoyable on a board rather than on skis because the weight transfer from front to back is a tad more melodic than the side-to-side transfer of skiing—in my opinion. It's only a personal preference, but one that I stand by, and should you end up mastering both sports, you too will find a love for one or the other.

Ah yes, the tricker chairlift process! Getting on a lift in skis is very (literally) straightforward. You coast in, through the line, facing forward, and sitting down. With snowboarding, things can get dicey. I myself have fallen numerous times during this process. When reaching the bottom of a slope, a boarder will have to unlatch one of their feet from its bindings. The distinction of the foot depends on whether they ride regular or goofy, but once they have, they'll have one foot free and one still attached to their board. When you're gliding through the line, you'll have your back foot pushing you along as well as keeping you stable. Once you approach the front, you'll ready yourself for the chair by remaining sideways, only to sit down as the chair takes you off your feet. Now you'll be along for the ride with your board hanging sideways. The tricky part here is getting off the lift. You reposition yourself as though you are going to ride down the slope. Although your back foot won't be attached to your board, a sticky pad in the middle known as a stomp pad will be where you place your foot as you ride down the mini-slope of the off-ramp. Keep your wits about you because this is where most wipeouts can occur involving the chairlift. Simply maintain your balance as best you can and try not to flail your arms or use people to either one of your sides to keep yourself upright (unless you have willing friends to do so).

Tip 81: It's All in the Hips—Perfecting the "Box Out" Method (Part I)

In skiing, we had our medial and lateral edges. We learned the importance of the pizza and french fry methods and how we direct ourselves by pointing our tips. Perfecting the ski turn is much easier because of the body's natural disposition to point our toes as a means of stopping. However, when it comes to snowboarding, it is far more difficult and complex. It also happens to be *the* most important aspect of boarding. Applying lateral pressure when turning or stopping on skis feels comfortable because we can put so much pressure on our edges when we're sideways. You can lean into it so hard, and it doesn't feel as scary or suspicious. Boarding is far more intimidating because of the innate fear of falling forwards or backward; because of this, mastering your turn is a crucial component in your journey. We've already talked about the heel/toe relationship, so I want you to remember that when considering what I'm about to tell you. Think of the power you disperse when you lean one way or the other and how we're going to transfer that power with the use of our hips. Thankfully, they're among one of the stronger muscles in the body, and they're what you'll need to perfect the turns. This is what brings us to something I dubbed the "Box Out" method; a kinesthetic learning style that I created to help my good friend learn when we were on our trip to Breckenridge many years ago.

Tip 82: It's All in the Hips—Perfecting the "Box Out" Method (Part II)

Without revealing my friend's real name, from this point forward, we will refer to him as "Joe." Joe is one of my best friends from college and has always been a natural athlete. He spent most of his early years as an avid participant in track and field events while sharing a deep love for basketball. When we first arrived at Breckenridge (as I admitted earlier), I was a little too keen to explore the mountain before I put on my teaching hat. After some time and a few "try this" and "you can do this" types of support, I finally came to the mature decision that it was time to help my friend and be a little more selfless. The selfish part was when I decided it would be a good idea to take him up a fairly steep blue square trail for his first-ever experience. *Awful idea.* He was none too pleased, but after food, lunchtime drinks, and some "liquid courage," we were ready to get back out there. For the next two hours, I tried everything that I could to attempt some sort of teaching breakthrough. I'd brought up the heel/toe relationship, the pumping of the heels and toes separately, the bending of the knees, and the counterbalance of the arms. Nothing was breaking through until I remembered a moment from my time as a camp counselor where I was able to relate to a camper of mine. I used a soccer metaphor to help him tack (turn upwind) in a sailboat. The visual metaphor helped him to understand what needed to be done. The same occurred with Joe. I kept trying to think of something, *something* that would help him, and finally, like a lightbulb, it came to me. Initiating and executing a turn in snowboarding is frighteningly similar to boxing someone out on the basketball court. As I said, it's all in the hips. From that breakthrough onward, we indeed had progressed.

Tip 83: It's All in the Hips—Perfecting the "Box Out" Method (Part III)

When one is on a basketball court, dribbling down to score, there may be an instance where they'll be confronted by a defender. In such a moment, they'll come to a stop. It may be that they'll keep dribbling the ball or stop entirely to pick it up, looking for someone to pass it to or an angle to shoot the ball. When this happens, you aren't allowed to move your feet. All you can do is pivot off of the one stationary foot by boxing out the defender who is covering you. Think of your plant foot as your downhill foot and your movable foot as your uphill foot. When riding either your heel or toe edge, and approaching your turn, think of your downhill foot as your pivot foot. Let's say you're riding your toe edge: you're going to leave your "center" and lean forward just a little bit so that you can have control in initiating your turn. Then—much like your mobile foot when boxing out on the court—your uphill foot is going to swing a full 180 degrees around, transitioning smoothly to your heel edge for your ride towards the other edge of the slope. The initiation of the turn will see you leaning slightly forward, but midway through your execution, you'll feel yourself leaning back slightly to apply pressure to the opposing edge. Easier said than done, try and use this visual when you're practicing because if you're anything like Joe, perhaps this learning style can be of some benefit to you. Instructors may try and communicate lessons on the mountain through styles like these, and they're extremely helpful if you've hit a roadblock.

Tip 84: Directional vs. True Twin

Similar to skis and their variants, snowboards also have different stylings that adhere to different riders' preferences. Most commonly, snowboards are broken up into true twins or some form of a directional twin. True twins are akin to twin tips in skis. They're the most suited for beginners and offer a playful, carefree style of riding that gives you some edge but makes it more pleasant and forgiving to ride. Directional twins involve niche styles of riding, most often powder boards. While skis and boards have their differences in regards to their purpose, they do share some similarities and alignments. Yes, the true twin boards are like twin tip skis; however, they can be made for some serious carving and hard turning. My board, the Jones I've spoken of, is a true twin and so stiff you could carve a diamond with it. It would be the board equivalent of racer skis. My first board was the 420, and that thing was about as powder-driven, directional tip as it gets. More for playing around than taking any serious Ss down the mountain. While it's not entirely important which you choose, versions of both are acceptable for beginners.

Tip 85: Additional Assembly May Be Required

While what I'm about to discuss may not entirely be "necessary reading," it is something I think beginners could benefit from because of the safety it can provide. As always, wear a helmet, especially to help with those backward falls, but other important pieces of random gear could otherwise prevent further injury. Something I used in the first two years was essentially a tailbone protector. It was a set of padded compression shorts that covered my thighs, butt, and tailbone in the center. It softened many blows I took and frankly may have saved me from a busted tailbone at several points. It also offered a good deal of added warmth which was pretty nice as well. The second thing is something that all you skateboarders may be familiar with and fond of...wrist guards. They fit nicely underneath a good pair of gloves or mittens and have stopped my 250-pound self from faceplanting in the snow without breaking my wrists. They're exceptionally strong and are hardly noticed underneath the rest of what you're wearing. There have been times later in my experience where I've ridden without them, fallen hard enough, and believed to have broken my wrists, so it doesn't hurt (literally) to have something like this in your arsenal. The last one is a fairly common item that I briefly mentioned, the stomp pad. Some riders don't like to use them because they don't want to have anything permanently stuck on their board. I find it very useful because it helps me keep balance. They're fairly cheap and inexpensive, so it's not too much sweat off your back. These are only suggestions, not must-be's, so take them into consideration! You may find that it helps.

Tip 86: My First Time (Part I)

Much like the last chapter and my first experience skiing, my first time snowboarding was an experience that I've always held close to my heart. For many years of skiing, I'd wanted to learn how to board, and in some instances, I even tried. Through three separate professional lessons, over the course of five winters, I learned a lot of valuable information and how to begin my new passion, but it never took. I always got so frustrated with myself and the fact that it was too hard to learn. I even walked away from two of the lessons. I simply couldn't figure out how to make this transition to a completely different sport. This all changed very quickly, however. One lovely winter, my last before college, I took my high school best friend (whom I'll name Bob) to my home in Maine and the mountain I grew up on, Shawnee Peak. I figured that a good taste of home could perhaps spark my interest yet again and maybe even stick. Not but a few days after New Year's did my friend and I arrive so our fun could begin. New snowfall made the mountain ripe for the pickin', and he and I were more than ready to take on the slopes. We arrived later in the evening, just in time to feast on the *wonderful* lobster mac n' cheese my mom had prepared. If there's one thing that Maine has (aside from more coastline than California—true fact, feel free to look it up), it has *the* best lobster in the world. It was the perfect meal for us leading into our first day, where patience was tested, and fun was had.

Tip 87: My First Time (Part II)

Since Bob had never skied before, he didn't have any gear to speak of. Thankfully, we provided him with all the warm clothing and outer shell gear he needed. The next part was renting his boots and skis, whereas poles were something we did have extras of. After getting him fitted for his boots, we found a nice rental pair of skis for him to try out. We made our way to the two-seater chair lift designated for the bunny slope. Shawnee is not a big mountain by any stretch, only about 2,000 of vertical incline to speak of. It has the two-seater bunny lift, the four-person quad lift that leads to all blue square trails, and then the main triple seater that reaches the summit. A fun part about the summit triple is that it has a midway drop point that will take you down the green and blue trails from a higher point. If you do take the chair to the summit, you not only get breathtaking views of the White Mountains (most notably Mount Washington on a clear enough day), but you have access to the black diamonds and double black diamonds available to you. While we didn't reach the summit for a couple of days, we intelligently began on the smallest slopes possible, ones that are nearly flat (at least to someone like me). Bob was in for a semi-rude awakening. From the moment we rode off the chair lift, chaos was not far behind us.

Tip 88: My First Time (Part III)

With perhaps the world's quickest verbal crash course in "How to Ski" told on the chairlift ride up (which lasts around eight minutes), I overconfidently thought that it would have been enough for him to grasp the concept...boy, was I wrong. The second we touched down at the top, he seemed to have lost all coordination entirely. His feet completely went pizza inward and soon out from under him. After the lift operator stopped the chair from moving, I promptly helped him to his feet. I took us to the side for a moment assured him that I would go down the trail a little bit, leave my gear, and walk back up to assist him. After returning, I walked him through the pizza, french fry, and leaning forward as best I could. We tried and tried, but his biggest issue, in the beginning, was keeping upright. The yearning to lean back was easily his biggest fault, and try as he did, it was the main obstacle of the first day. We didn't see much past the bunny slope that opening day, but he was determined to get better, and I was ready to give my patience another try. Day two came around quickly, but my patience did not. I kept trying to help and counsel him, and although there was some minor improvement, it was still a struggle for him. Around lunchtime is when I had my little epiphany, however. I said to myself, "If he's gonna suffer and be falling on his butt all day, I might as well do the same." The time had finally come for me to walk this path yet again and see if they yearn to learn outmatched my stubborn, hardheadedness. The beginning was *not* pretty. I mean, I was falling left and right. It was absolutely *brutal*. Every turn attempt was a borderline shattering of my kneecaps or unholy bending of my wrists. A toe or heel was certain to catch whether it was the attempted left or right turn. It didn't matter though, because Bob was "beefing it" right alongside me.

Tip 89: My First Time (Part IV)

We eventually made our way off of the bunny slope (thank God) and up to the blue chair, quad lift. This is personally my favorite lift at Shawnee because of the versatility it has in that part of the mountain. You have your steeper chutes and your wider groomers, and we figured the more liberal green circles from that summit would serve as a good "upping of the ante" for us. Somehow, somewhere along the way, we both seemed to "click" into place. It was wild! Beginning of day three and we were already off to a great start. There had been about five inches of fresh powder, so it made the falls a little bit more tolerable. We'd found our edges and were surprisingly taking our turns nicely. He had nailed the pizza/french fry while I had figured out my turns and toe edges. I then went on to avoid my—not created at the time—self advice of not biting off more than I can chew. I preceded to do so by the fourth day. We ended up taking on one of the longer and steeper blue square trails on the mountain. A personal favorite of mine when it comes to the casual big S. As they say in the South, I got a little too big for my britches. At this point, I made several turns down the mountain without falling, so I thought it would be a *great* idea to try and film myself while riding this glorious, massive trail. This was early on when smartphones didn't have the best recording abilities, so the video was a little grainy, but wow, did it provide some entertaining content. I was gliding through a couple of turns, all was well, and I ended up catching the gnarliest of heel edges, followed by roughly three backflips and some hilarious grunts in between. The pain was only made better by the laughs that Bob and I were having after the fact. We learned our lesson though, and completely humbled ourselves back down to some easier greens.

Tip 90: My First Time (Part V)

By the end of the week, our mutual progress was far more than I had ever expected it would be. Bob was making amazingly precise turns and keeping his skis parallel, while I had managed to do several runs without even falling. Like the indoctrinating days in Aspen of old, I had found in me a new passion. This idea that was born in me hit ten times as hard as skiing. It may have been because I was older and a bit more aware, or maybe it was simply that I had discovered a completely new way to enjoy being a place that I've known all my life. It was like the blinders had been taken off, and I was seeing the mountain in an entirely new light. It truly rocked my world. A decade of asking for ski gear at Christmastime became an obsession with the boarding lifestyle. It was manic! I was so enthralled with the culture, history, and greats. I immersed myself into the research of brands and what kinds of boards, boots, and bindings I'd want to buy. I looked into finding new goggles and oversized hoodies for good measure. I simply couldn't get enough. It influenced every bit of being on the mountain from that point on. I even stopped skiing for a few years to master this new craft. Having gone through two snowboards already, I want another at this point just so I have a nice backup to work with on the more powder-induced days.

Chapter Review:

- Master the heel/toe. It is the beginning and the end of your journey as a snowboarder and will only lead to happiness once harnessed.
- Perfect the "box out" and earn your turns. Feel it in your hips and lower back; the more power you exert, the more precise your turns.
- Accept the fact that you are going to be sore and bruised at the end of the day. Teach yourself how to fall, and know that it just might hurt a little. Hey, it's half the fun!
- Bend your damn knees and find your center! Stand tall with one or both legs and accept the fact that there's going to be unwanted chaos abound if you do.
- Take it slow. Know your place in the beginning, because if you don't humble yourself, I promise you that the mountain certainly will.

Chapter 4: Planning Your Adventure!

Where to Go, What to Pack, and How to Do It

East Coast vs. West Coast

Tip 91: The East

It may not have been where my journey started, but my God, this is where I grew up. I Have spent more time riding trails in the East than in any other part of the country. For me, the greatest thing about the East, more specifically the Northeast, is how close together so many mountains are. From Vermont, across to New Hampshire, on to Maine. The concentration of high-quality mountains here is enough to leave you discovering new places for ten lifetimes. The beauty of it lies in the variety of the types of mountains you'll encounter. They don't reach the same types of heights as they do in the West (roughly half the size), but there are a lot that reach somewhere between the 4-5,000-foot range, and this offers some great benefits. Altitude doesn't affect you one bit. Sure, you're a little under a mile or so above sea level on some of the peaks, but even then, you don't notice how high up you are, and you can still maintain reasonable breathing patterns. This isn't always a problem out West, but it can be bothersome at times when you're tired and out of breath. Probably the biggest benefit of East skiing is that at no time while you are riding on those mountains will you be in danger of an avalanche. Places in the West get so much snowfall, but that's not the issue. The overall height of the mountains is indicative of how dangerous they can be. The high snowfall coupled with high peaks makes for dangerous snow buildup. While there is tremendous snowfall in the East, the mountains aren't big enough for such a buildup to come crashing down. Not to mention, the

Northeast has some of the highest recorded windspeeds in the world, particularly atop Mount Washington, so a great deal of snow gets blown around and doesn't get as packed in.

In Vermont, you have mountains like Stowe, Okemo, and my personal favorite: Killington, otherwise known as the "Beast of the East." This is where you'll find some of the biggest mountains New England has to offer. Remember what I said about high winds? These mountains will have you understanding the meaning of "icy runs" in no time. Personally, I've never had an issue with it because I like to carve, but these places are something out of a fairytale. Vermont as a whole is such a unique place to be. The towns and cities are beautiful, and my goodness, you'll never find better maple syrup anywhere in the world; anything maple syrup enthused, really. Maple candied, maple bacon, maple-smoked turkey, and beyond. It adds a real winter wonderland type of vibe to the place.

New Hampshire has a bit of a different feel to it. It's a love child combination of cultures mixed from Vermont and Maine. It doesn't feel as "free-spirited" as Vermont does, more of an old-school, blue-collar remnant of a time in America long past. It gives "small-town America" its name, and my God (like the rest of New England), it is *beautiful*. There isn't as much in the vein of larger mountains, but some fun ones remain in Bretton Woods, Loon Mountain, and North Conway. Little towns and a variety of great local restaurants are spread out through the long back roads that are laid into the White Mountain range. In most parts of New Hampshire, on the clearest of days, you can actually see Mount Washington gleaming in the distance, in all of its snow-capped glory. It truly is a sight to behold and is one of the state's most iconic images. When people think of New Hampshire, it is thoughts of this mountain that they are reminded of. A true natural wonder.

Tip 92: *Maine*

Finally, we come to the place I call home: Maine. Keep in mind this next paragraph *may* very well be biased because of my deeply rooted love for the place, but I assure you that everything I say comes from the heart, so I do mean it. I've always referred to Maine as "God's Country," not because I am a religious man, but because of the divine beauty that this landscape inspires. It's truly something. A long, beautiful coastline stretching for thousands of miles, with even more thousands of mountains coating its interior. You'll find the best lobster in the world, immaculate clam chowder, and a Maine dessert specialty: whoopie pies! The amount that this place offers is matched only by a few. It also offers a wide variety of places to shred fresh powder and crispy groomers.

Beginning only an hour north of the miniature metroplex that is the always satisfying Portland (by the way, the *original* Portland, sorry to all you Oregonians), lies the beautiful little town of Bridgton. Across the causeway of Moose Pond, right on Route 302, sits the entrance to Shawnee Peak. Although it is a relatively small mountain, it is still mighty. Having been around for eighty-four years, Shawnee has seen immense improvements to its landscape and has constantly been improved during its time. Many of those upgrades have happened during my eighteen years cruising through its trails. It's an amazing place that I recommend to any beginner or expert. Fun will be had, and great food will be eaten at the Blizzard Pub located in the base lodge. Roughly an hour north is one of the biggest resorts in Maine: Sunday River. This place is *massive*, with eight separate peaks and hundreds of acres to explore; there is so much to do. I mentioned my experience earlier with their expert trails, so it should be a hint at the wide variety of trails this mountain can offer. It is certainly one of the bigger mountains in the state, so a single day there will not guarantee that you'll see all of it—believe me, I've tried. However, the cast iron brisket mac n' cheese at their main lodge is a delicacy any famished rider should try.

Finally, we have the *big boy* of Maine: Sugarloaf. You thought that Sunday River was big? Sugarloaf's acreage almost doubles it. It is also the most West Coast reminiscent mountain that the state has in store. Located about two and a half hours north of Shawnee, its massive backcountry runs offer awe-inspiring glades that seemingly never end, in addition to a couple hundred groomed trails as well. Although it is a bit out of the way in terms of travel, it is widely considered among, if not the best in the state, and is certainly a stop you should make in your adventures. In closing, New England is an illustrious section of the country where the beauty of its landscape is matched only by how close and proximate it all is. Dozens of places all within hardly one hundred miles of each other. Its personality and charm will keep you enamored for a long time if you let it.

Tip 93: The West

Although my love for the East is immense, it cannot even compare to the breadth and domain that the West holds. A lot of people—and this is pure conjecture—don't seem to understand just how massive the western United States is. I say that because during the several times in my life that I've driven coast to coast, I've gained perspective on just how mind-blowingly expansive the country is west of Dallas, Texas. Hundreds, thousands of miles of vast open skies, and a surprising amount of desert—south that is. Head a couple hundred, and again in some cases over a thousand miles north, and you'll see some of the biggest skiable mountains in the world. I could fill a hundred pages with what I know and a thousand with what I don't, but what I do know is that there are too many mountains and too little time to give proper credit to them all. A single mountain in Colorado alone could match the acreage of the entire Northeast. Among Washington, Oregon, California, Utah, Wyoming, Montana, Idaho, and of course Colorado, lie some of the biggest and best mountains in the world, waiting to be explored.

Saying the West is a different breed would be a gross understatement. In Vail, Colorado, a single trail is as big as Shawnee back in Maine. As a whole, it's something you have to see to believe. You could start your journey high up in the Pacific Northwest in Washington to see places like Mount Spokane or Crystal Mountain. A few hours south in Oregon, you'll find the likes of Hood Meadows and Mount Bachelor. The Northwest weather currents are the beginning of the entire Pacific water cycle, so the snowfall in the winter is only matched by its rainfall in the summer. The heavy precipitation allows for massive amounts of snow and some of the best powder riding in the nation.

While these states are reasonably sized, they do offer something similar to New England in that their mountains have nice proximity. The same cannot be said for its mega-state neighbors. Whether it's Sun Valley in central Idaho, Big Sky in southern Montana, my bucket list dream vacation of Jackson Hole in western Wyoming, or Park City in Utah, the northernmost parts of the country are going to show you sites that seem otherworldly. In truth, it's almost difficult to describe. While Colorado has an immense mountain highway connecting all the major mountains, say for a few, it all feels as though it's meshed together. You feel at altitude with the other mountains. In these states, however, the mountains stand far apart. When you reach a peak of any given one, the surroundings are made to feel so much bigger because of the isolation that they reside in. You can be atop a breathtaking peak, and a towering mountain miles away can seem like it's right in front of you. These are the types of mountains you visit if you want a spiritual experience, in my opinion. It's the kind of place that truly feels otherworldly. It would be the closest thing to a frozen alien planet I think that you can ever see in your life.

Next on our journey south is a place I've already spoken of at length, so I won't take up too much time with it. Of course, I'm talking about Colorado. The mountain highway that runs through the middle of the state will take you to all the classics. The greatest hits. Some of the world's most popular and revered slopes lay along this highway, from the aforementioned Breckenridge and Aspen to Vail, Keystone, and Steamboat. You won't run out of entertainment, and you certainly won't tire of the beautiful array of ski towns and villages to fill your off-mountain hours.

Finally, we have California: a clear-skied sunshine state in the South and a pristine natural landscape in the North. From the Redwoods to the shores of Lake Tahoe, Northern California is something else, and only a few hours from some of the biggest cities in the world, the best of both worlds. Lake Tahoe most specifically hosts a large number of some of the top-rated resorts in the country. Places like Northstar, Kirkwood, and Heavenly are just some of the highly regarded mountains that surround the lake. If you've never been, Lake Tahoe enormous. We're not talking "Top 10 in the US" or anything like that, but certainly enough to inspire an audible gasp. One of the best things about mountains is the lake and the broad views you get. There's something particularly illuminating when you're riding down a trail that sits above the tree line, looking at some of the bluest water you'll ever see in a seemingly never-ending expanse.

Big Bear is probably the best bang for your buck skiing I've witnessed in California. The crazy thing is: it's in Southern California and only about two and a half hours east of Los Angeles. It's a relatively small mountain, all things concerned, but for the price of admission, and the proximity to the city, it's tough to beat.

If you're from the area, it's a great weekend getaway with a night or two in an Airbnb.

Tip 94: Mammoth

When I initially arrived in California, Big Bear was my first ski experience in the state. I went once for a day trip and once again for a double overnight sometime after. Six months into my time here, I planned a long weekend trip to Northern California, but not to Lake Tahoe—no—I went to a place that had been in my mind for years. A place locals cherish and travelers flock to, *Mammoth*. Mammoth Mountain is roughly a five-hour drive north of Los Angeles, and let me tell you; it is worth it.

There are few mountains that I have experienced in my life that have given me the ride that this place did. We arrived at a little loft/condo we had rented and had two wonderful days of mountain time ahead of us. This was MLK Weekend in 2019, so it was in the prime of winter, and my goodness, the conditions were beautiful. On our first day there, you couldn't see a cloud in the sky. The mountain had received about half a foot the night before, so the groomers were packed down beautifully for the day. Oddly enough, for a Saturday, there were no lines—I kid you not—the lifts were clear, and we practically had the mountain to ourselves! After the long day of winding runs, we decided to wind down ourselves in town. The village has numerous great wine bars and cheeseries for the avid charcuterie consumer, as well as some great steak houses.

That night, around 5 PM, the snow began to fall, and it did not stop for the next forty-eight hours. Early Sunday morning, we were getting dressed and ready to head to the mountain, and it was a complete whiteout. It was a true thing of beauty. You could hardly see ten feet in front of you, but we knew we were in for something great. It was also the first time I knew I'd be able to try out my freshly acquired Faction skis. I'd never experienced fresh powder like this in my life. I mean, I was knee-deep in this stuff for about 90% of the day. It was heaven. The amazing thing about snowfall like that is the silence it brings. Snow absorbs so much of the sound around you until the only thing you hear is the light fall of snowflakes onto the surface. It's one of the most serene and peaceful things you can witness and a true pleasure. To make things better, the AFC and NFC Championship games were taking place later in the day, which we ended up viewing in the base lodge. Amazing drink and food selection made for wonderful viewing of the games. Not to mention it was the final stop in the playoffs before watching my Patriots win another ring! Any time you get the chance, take the trip to Mammoth. Unfortunately, I didn't have near enough time to experience the full amount that the town and mountain have to offer, but it's a stop that I recommend on anyone's journey.

Tip 95: Be Prepared, Know What to Plan For

I've had my fair share of trip planning, especially ski trip planning, and the one thing I cannot stress enough is to *plan ahead*. Nothing will behoove you more than having a fully laid out week where you know your sleeping situation, (possible) rental situation, and maybe some nice dinner reservations in between. Book your living situation at a minimum of three months in advance and six months in advance if it's during the holidays. Something to consider is a third-party rental app like Airbnb or Vrbo, but if you have enough of the money, it never hurts to stay at a resort. In the Northeast, you can expect very cute New England-style cottages that are perhaps for rent. In contrast, you may find wonderful modern apartments or condominiums for a reasonable price in the West. Unlike decently priced and booked ahead of time rentals, resorts will usually run you a decent dollar no matter what time of year you book. That being said, if you want to live your ski life in absolute luxury and pamper, there are plenty of places to seek out. If you're renting equipment, always remember to search for combination rentals, as I've said before. You'll save a buck, and they'll usually let you extend your time renting if you like. *The big* thing to avoid (except for once in a while should a fine dish come along) is mountain food. Don't let them distract you with the cafeteria-style lineup or some of the nicer places they may have for food. It's a trap. The food is nine out of ten times *SO good*, and it is also nine out of ten times wildly overpriced. If you can, pack a lunch and some snacks. Nothing crazy, nothing that necessarily needs heating, just simple stuff. Protein bars, sandwiches, maybe a fruit or two. Don't let me dissuade you from a cup of clam chowder or a hot and ready slice of pepperoni. Just try to space it out sometimes if you don't want to spend too much. A final thing would also be to pre-purchase your ski passes. It makes life much easier. Nowadays, you can simply pre-pay for a card, pick it up, and have a certain number of access days loaded up.

For me, aside from the darn thing I'm riding down a mountain on, *the* single biggest essential that I have to bring on the slopes with me is my headphones. I don't need music while I ride, but hot damn, does it enhance the experience. Think of it like this: would you go to the gym without headphones? No. Would you go for a run without music? Probably not (and for those of you that do—I fear you—because that is crazy to me!). Tuning into your favorite playlist can make a mountain experience unforgettable. Sometime in the future, you may hear a song again and be immediately transported back to the mountain, to that one moment in time where you felt bliss and happiness while experiencing something beautiful.

Tip 96: Après Ski

Here, we have a fun one. This is for all of the twenty-one-and-over crowd. A term coined by the French in their corner of the Alps, Après Ski, refers specifically to a social event held on the mountain after a day of skiing, usually drinks in the lodge. In today's world, it's become better known as having a few at lunch or at different points throughout the day. I mean, hey, it's vacation after all! Numerous places in the East and West have added locations throughout their mountains that will serve you on the slopes. It's one thing to have a nice beer in the base lodge at the bottom, but 9,000 feet up on the mountain? Halfway down a run? Tough to beat that feeling. It's a fun and refreshing way for you and your friends or family to treat yourselves. As I've said before, a little liquid courage can go a very long way when you're unsure of yourself! While keeping that in mind, know your limits. *Never* drink too much on the mountain because it can lead to a serious injury, especially in the West at high altitudes. If I haven't mentioned it yet, altitude can affect a lot of things.

Tip 97: Dealing with Altitude

While you won't deal with this sort of issue in the East, it's certainly something you'll experience in the West since almost all mountains you'll find there have bases that are somewhere above 9,000 feet above sea level. When you reach altitudes like that, there are a couple of things you'll notice first. You may walk up the stairs quickly, carrying your gear, and you'll find yourself out of breath. You may even be driving up into the mountains, only a mile above sea level, when you start to notice that it's a little harder to breathe. The higher you go, the scarcer oxygen becomes, which can be tough for someone who isn't as athletically inclined. I (in my less out-of-shape moments) have been hit with altitude problems at times. That's not the only thing you can feel; altitude sickness is like food poisoning that sucks more and simply won't go away. Trust me; you don't want it. The key to avoiding this is preparing your body and cardiovascular system for the change you will experience. Constant and steady hydration is part of it as well, which brings me to my next point. Alcohol will hit *much* harder when you're two miles above sea level, so if you've felt the effects of the altitude aggressively, maybe lay off the juice for the first few days until you fully adjust.

Tip 98: Packing a Backpack

If you're like me, and someone who owns their own boots, you'll bring a boot bag to the mountain. Boot bags are amazing not just for your sturdy outer footwear but for what folks like myself bring in it. It holds my helmet, goggles, beanies, facemasks, extra layers of any kind (I like to be prepared), extra water bottles, and of course, my mountain backpack. A mountain backpack traditionally can hold smaller items that you can (and should) take on the mountain. Like the one I own, many of these will act as a Camelback-styled water pouch with a tube that you can sip your water from. It'll keep you hydrated all day and make for an excellent safety measure to battle dehydration. You can also keep your snacks in there in case you get the munchies sometime throughout the day. I also like to keep a personal charger for my phone with me should it die unexpectedly. There is no greater buzzkill than your music giving out on you in the middle of a run. Handwarmers are also an option for those windy, subzero days up there. On occasion, for those who are of age, it never hurts to have a nip or two of your favorite liquor tucked away to perk up your senses and keep you warm. Having a backpack can be helpful, but it is not helpful in some small cases. The only aspect that makes a backpack somewhat of a burden is when you're on the chairlift, but since a majority of your day won't be spent there, you needn't worry.

Tip 99: Creating an Itinerary

While I've mentioned that it's important to understand what your plan is for whatever vacation you may indulge in, it doesn't hurt to have a day-to-day itinerary. I'm not saying it has to be the minute-by-minute plan every second of your day type, just something that generalizes what you'll be doing. It's a fair assumption that most of your day (at the very least, 8:00 AM-4:00 PM) is going to be spent on the mountain. However, throwing in a couple of local activities can't hurt. Depending on the region, some mountains host certain fun events for the visiting rider to attend. Occasionally, certain brands will host demo days where they offer demos of their equipment while giving out free stuff for people who partake. On other occasions for things during the holiday season or later on for spring skiing on St. Patrick's Day, they'll have themed dress events where you'll see people riding down the mountain in outfits that fit the seasonal event. The bottom line is this: take time out of your days to explore your surroundings. There is so much that these villages have to offer, and I bet my bottom dollar that they hold things that will only amplify your travel experience.

Chapter Review:

- Understand the geography. Do your research, and learn about places that would fit your wants.
- Let loose a little, but not too loose! Check yourself before you wreck yourself.
- Understand your body and how it may react being two miles above sea level.
- Plan (and pack) accordingly! Nothing is more frustrating than being at the mountain and realizing you've left something at home.
- Think ahead, plan, and create a detailed schedule so you can use every glorious minute to its fullest on your journey.

Chapter 5: Congrats! You've Reached the End

Take What You've Learned and Apply It

Tip 100: Here's the End of the Book, but Not the End of Your Journey

We've made it! One hundred tips later, and I think you may be ready to hit the slopes. However, that's not the end of it; you *must* apply yourself. This passion is time and money-consuming. You'll spend a lot of both while chasing your curiosity, but my God, do I encourage it. I *want* you to try, and I *want* you to see that a little time and patience can go a long way. It's a beautiful couple of sports and an even more beautiful lifestyle, but it takes some earning. You have to work your way up and find the talent inside you. I hope that this guide has been helpful and that it inspires you to continuously improve, get better, and inspire others. I wish nothing but the best and good luck to you all.

Tip 101: Have Fun!

There isn't much more to it than that. *Have fun*. Enjoy yourself. This is the experience and journey of a lifetime. Take it step by step, and enjoy the ride. There's nothing better.

About the Author

Blake Randall is an avid skier and snowboarder whose twenty years of experience have taken him to all corners of America in a seemingly never-ending journey to discover new peaks to conquer. He has been hitting the slopes since the tender age of seven after a trip to Aspen, Colorado, ignited a passion deep inside of him. Ever since, he has striven to improve his skills and explore as many mountains as possible, even teaching friends along the way. There has yet to be a place that he hasn't enjoyed because he always finds the beauty, satisfaction, and uniqueness in each place he visits.

HowExpert publishes how to guides by everyday experts. Visit HowExpert.com to learn more.

Recommended Resources

- HowExpert.com – Quick 'How To' Guides on All Topics from A to Z by Everyday Experts.
- HowExpert.com/free – Free HowExpert Email Newsletter.
- HowExpert.com/books – HowExpert Books
- HowExpert.com/courses – HowExpert Courses
- HowExpert.com/clothing – HowExpert Clothing
- HowExpert.com/membership – HowExpert Membership Site
- HowExpert.com/affiliates – HowExpert Affiliate Program
- HowExpert.com/jobs – HowExpert Jobs
- HowExpert.com/writers – Write About Your #1 Passion/Knowledge/Expertise & Become a HowExpert Author.
- HowExpert.com/resources – Additional HowExpert Recommended Resources
- YouTube.com/HowExpert – Subscribe to HowExpert YouTube.
- Instagram.com/HowExpert – Follow HowExpert on Instagram.
- Facebook.com/HowExpert – Follow HowExpert on Facebook.
- TikTok.com/@HowExpert – Follow HowExpert on TikTok.

Made in United States
Troutdale, OR
12/10/2024

26187797R00063